POETICALLY ECLECTIC

JOHN SHILLITO

authorHOUSE®

AuthorHouse™ UK Ltd.
1663 Liberty Drive
Bloomington, IN 47403 USA
www.authorhouse.co.uk
Phone: 0800.197.4150

Published by AuthorHouse   09/29/2014

ISBN: 978-1-4969-9217-8 (sc)
ISBN: 978-1-4969-9218-5 (e)

POETICALLY ECLECTIC

a motley collection of verse

all the following poems are the work of
John Shillito

The poems have been printed in
alphabetic order
since there is no theme
Each poem starts on a new page
Sometimes this leaves large
blank spaces so
the best companion for this book
is a pencil (and possibly an eraser)

Add a verse
Improve the original
Write something new
Add an illustration

There are ten
poems at the end
from my previous book

PAWPRINTS
ON MY
HEART
Published 2013
and
FOUR SHORT STORIES
Contact
Scooby@Pawprints-on-my-heart.com

TABLE OF CONTENTS

A Full Heart 1
The Art Of Living 3
Artistic Temperament 4
Beware Ye Tyrants 5
The Blind Lord Of The Underpass 6
Born To Be Wild 11
Budgie Jumping 13
Built With Love 14
Bye, Polar 15
Concreted Impressions 17
Crocodile Wood 18
Crying Country 19
Dance Eternal 20
Desolate 21
Diesel And Cow 31
Disco Len 33
Do Not Bug Us 35
Does She Think Of Me 36
Dogs Of War 37
Dour 38
Draconian Nurture 39
The Dragon Hunters 41
The Dragon Of Autumn 43
Dragonheart 45
Dunn's Brown Cow 48
Earthbound 49
Eddies Fireworks 50
Edmund The Dancing Kangaroo 53
Emotional Outburst 55
Enablement 56
Endless Night 57
Eternal Weave 58
Fallible 60
First Harvest 61
Fishing With Ferdinand 62
Flyin Amber 64
Flying Home 65

Frozen Evolution 66
Gypsy Heart 67
Harriet The Hornet 68
Haunted Glades 69
Healing 71
Hear The Devil 72
Heartwood 73
Heroic Indifference 74
Honour Of The Regiment 76
I Wish That There Were Dragons 77
Imaginative Gardening 78
Infantisuicide 79
Inseparable 80
It Bee Spring 81
It's Not Cricket! 82
Just Another Birthday 83
Just Words 84
Kite 85
Lament 86
Legacy 87
Liberation 89
A Lincolnshire Welcome 90
Logical Argument 91
Looking Forward 92
Love Eternal 93
Lovely Weather Today 94
Marion The Molehunter 96
Memories 103
Messenger 104
Midnight Passions 106
Mind Games 107
Moonstruck 108
Multitudes Spring Forth 109
The Naming Of Deities 110
Nightmare 111
One True Thing 112
Pack 113
Passing Strangers 114
Peewit 115
Peregrine 116
Poppy Parade 117

Reactions 118
Dark Knight (Redemption) 119
Riding With The Angels 120
Rite Of Way 121
Run For Your Lives 122
The Saga Of Sid The Sardine 123
Santa's Postmen 124
Save A Space 125
The Scale Of A Dragon 126
The Seance 127
Simple Solutions 128
Sinner? 129
Sisters Of Mercy 130
The Skies Of Lincolnshire 131
Slithery Snake's Snack 132
Song Of A Life 134
Sorrow 135
Starman 136
The Guns (Dance With The Devil) 137
The Others 138
Tideline 143
Tiger Toes 144
Time Of Colours 145
Tommy And His 303 147
Transfrogmification 148
Traveller's Tales 149
Turnover 150
Universal Indifference 151
Victim 152
Victorious 153
Visage 155
The Voice Of Snow 156
We Know Best 157
Wear It With Pride 158
What Will Be Your Answer? 160
Winter's Holiday 161

A FULL HEART

It's the howl of a lonely mountain wolf,
calling for his mate
The sobbing of a woman,
when her man is out too late
The tremble in a lovers hand,
on a sweetheart's garden gate
Or its the snarl of pain, as once again,
frustration is your fate

It's the moonlight on your lover's hair,
the love light in their eyes
Or the fear and desperation as at last,
too late, you realise
The moan as your heart tears apart,
the scream as all hope dies
When you learn they love another,
and this is your last goodbye

It's the promise of warmth and comfort
at the end of a winding trail
The hope that always beckons
at the end of the shining rails
It's the futures that are waiting
if you follow your Yukon trail
Or the numb despair, as all dreams fade,
and all ambitions fail

It's that feeling when your children play,
laughing, in the sun
It's the wind across the open plains,
a horse that was born to run
The hound that bounds to greet you
when the dreary day is done
And it's loving arms to hold you,
being told you are the one

AFGHAN GIRLIES

(please read it all before screaming racist?)

When an Afghan girlie smiles
it don't mean she wants to flirt
It means she's got yer cornered
and you know its gonna hurt

Though they flutter their eyelashes
and looks demure and sweet
If they beckon from an alley
keep yer boots firm on the street

Them girls does lots o' chopping
afore they gets to be a wife
and just before the wedding
Afghan girlies gets a knife

The scraping drives you crazy
when they sharpens up the blade
But when it stops you're sorry
as yer watch the corporal flayed

Then its snick snick and chop
on yer fingers an yer toes
an' all the time yer wonderin'
what's next when they all goes

They makes yer scream and wriggle
then they cuts a little more
an' yer don't want to be lookin'
at what's lyin' on the floor

I wed an Afghan girlie
you can't find a better wife
but I still gets the shivers
when she sharpens up 'er knife!

THE ART OF LIVING

The first life I remember was within my family
It was noisy, bright and cheerful, I recall it fuzzily
Parents, teachers, many others, issuing direction
It wasn't really mine, just one splash or an inflection

I flew the nest to you, my love, heart and soul ablaze
Bright and clear my memory, of those halcyon days
Whenever I would falter, your hand was there, on mine
to add your special hue, or to straighten out a line

Then you faded and were gone, to fast to understand
My picture lost coherence, without your helping hand
Now all is silent monochrome, carved in cold, hard stone
OUR life together is over, and now MY life begins - alone

ARTISTIC TEMPERAMENT

Another party, another girl, another aching dawn
Coffee, fags and insults, then she or I have gone
Digs or squat or someone's pad, eat, crash again
Someone puked on Harry, somehow I get blamed

Dye my roots, re-dye the lot, shave or grow a beard?
Then I'd have to dye it too, not easy, so I've heard
Some different clothes, what sort of scene is it tonight?
Of course they're mine! - Tatty, cheap and very bright

Is that my phone? Oh no, its Beckie to complain
Gods! Is it Sunday? I forgot to visit little Sam again
Look at all the messages, from her and Dad and Mum
I wish they'd see its pointless, beating that old drum

I need my space and freedom, its what I'm all about
They say that I am just another lazy scrounging lout
But my muse needs inspiration. A drink? Another fag?
And my artistic muse would find a job a boring drag

BEWARE YE TYRANTS

Pale, delicate petals, so battered and bruised
Glimpsed briefly, only to be trampled and broken
Persisting, clinging, tenacious weed of the wastelands
Relentlessly uprooted, hacked, burned and poisoned

and still its roots persist, dig deeper, and endure
In quiet corners, those pale shoots will reappear
and though it may but seldom blossom
The scent will drive you wild, and haunt you forever

Ye believers, wherever there is fertile soil, plant it
Nurture it in secret groves, spread it's seed afar
and Beware, ye Tyrants, of freedom's fragile flower
For its thorns are sharp, and will one day bind you all

THE BLIND LORD
OF THE UNDERPASS

Three cheers for the Lord of the Underpass
Three cheers for his raggedy Hound
Three cheers for his pet Tarantula
Who is deaf, and won't hear a sound

The Voles suborned the Moles somehow
but the Lice just came for the ride
The Ferrets were totally outfoxed
while the Fox sneaked off to hide

They needed the Bats quite badly
to initiate all of the frenzy
This badly affected the starting date
the Bats were busy 'til Wednesday

The Stoats took little persuasion
They like mayhem, and being loud
The Rats turned up uninvited
a somewhat disorganised crowd

They worried a bit about Badger
so tough if it came to the crunch
Luckily, due to advancing years
Badger was 'out to lunch'

So at dusk on the fateful evening
the horde gathered in the gloom
The Voles indicated objectives
vaguely visible under the Moon

Sing out for the Lord of the Underpass
Howl for the brave Canine
Chant for the dancing Tarantula
But please try to keep it in time

The Bats' hypersonic screeching
sent the poor Dog nearly insane
The Lord stuffed Cockroaches in his ears
and hoped they'd come out again

The Moles moved much too slowly
They should not have led the attack
The Stoats just spread out sideways
but the Rats shoved hard at the back

Then Dog stepped up to defy them
a mountain of blood and heat
The Lice swept forward and over him
then settled down to eat

A disturbing sight for the Voles
So they paused, just to reassess
But the Rats and Stoats kept going
their formations becoming a mess

The Tarantula shinned up the wall
grabbed a Cockroach for a snack
Waited for just the right moment
and dropped onto the back of a Bat !!

When Tarantula nipped the Bat
he gave it a terrible shock
It looked back over its shoulder
and flew straight into the clock

This caused a complete disruption
All the crucial timings were lost
They asked each other for time checks
and everyone got very cross

The resident Fleas on Dog
launched a vicious counter-attack
the Rats started shrieking in terror
Fleas sometimes affect them like that

Meanwhile up aloft the Tarantula
was really having a ball
Leaping lithely from batback to Bat
and driving them into the wall

The Lord assessed the problem
as he quietly sat there, unheeded
The vibrations through the floor tiles
telling him how the battle proceeded

His white stick flicked at the Voles
surreptitiously sneaking by
Went blob blob blob very quickly
and he poked every Vole in the eye

The Voles had just recovered
from a trampling by Stoats and Rats
With one eye they now ran in circles
no-one had expected that

But despite their valiant resistance
The numbers were overwhelming
The Lord considered a desperate ploy
Burning the broom closet shelving!!

So praise the Lord of the Underpass
and praise his flea-bitten Dog
Praise his fat Tarantula
They are doing a fantastic job

Tarantula went inspirational
and turned the course of the fight
Steered his Bat into the sensor
and turned on the underpass light

The Moles recoiled from the brightness
made a break for a grill in the wall
They discovered it led to the sewer
Too late, as they'd started to fall

The remaining Bats peered dimly
at the shambles down below
"I think" one Bat yawned loudly
"It's Thursday, it's time to go"

The Tarantula hopped off his Bat
Got his Cockroach out for a bite
But the Dog was still in trouble
so he leapt back into the fight

The Fleas and Lice were still at it
as the Dog tried to bid them goodbye
Biting and scratching so madly
he nearly took out his own eye

Into the huge infestation
an eight-legged nightmare arrived
He gobbled them up like popcorn
not many of them survived

All praise the Lord of the Underpass
and praise his puissant Guard
Ignore the searching Tarantula
if he pulls your hair too hard

The Dog came back to his senses
His Sheepdog blood kicked in
He rounded the Stoats up smartly
and penned them in the bin

The army retreated in chaos
its doubtful they'll ever come back
The Fox and the Ferrets were waiting
One-eyed Voles - convenient snacks

The Moles all got home safely
but stay in their tunnels these days
Because of the smell no-one visits
and Voles stay well out of their way

The Stoats were eventually freed
and promised to mend their ways
They still like a little mayhem
but are quieter about it these days

So if it is quiet in your Park
and the creatures all crouch in fear
The Blind Lord of the Underpass
and his Cohorts are probably near

If you ever use that Underpass
and a white stick whacks your shin
Look compassionately at his plastic cup
Be grateful, and stick a quid in

Bless the Lord of the Underpass
Give his battered Hound a treat
and try not to step on Tarantula
Chasing Cockroaches round your feet !!

BORN TO BE WILD

She was born of the wind in the hemp and the flax
in the storm-tossed woods, in the heart of the tree
Out of the spirit of land and the sky
She was born to fly, she was born to be free

She danced like a maid at the coming of spring,
the first time her keel kissed the sea
But they trapped her inside the harbour
and they shackled her tight to the quay

Her planks were oiled and polished
'til the waters reflected their glow
They adorned her spars and slender masts
with their finest linens, as white as snow

Put a gilded figurehead on her prow
Strung a harness of hemp and steel
They praised her strength and her beauty
as they bound her to serve their will

And she slept for a while, complete at last
But a wind came up, a wind from the sea
and the storm-frets caressed her gently
Whispered of freedom, of what could be

She stirred at the sound of the waves on the shore
Their rhythm the beat of her heart
With the taste of spray and the cold salt air
The storm-winds tore her dreams apart

When the petrels swooped around her
Called to her soul, called her to flee
She tugged and fretted, then with one bound
She spread her wings, and was free!

Too late they tried to stop her,
as she fled past the harbour light
Into the teeth of the raging seas
She flew on the storm, out into the night

They still see her, slipping past them,
like a ghost in the dead of night
Or out on some distant horizon,
wings spread in glorious flight

But a fortunate few have seen her,
as she always was meant to be
Riding the crests of the storm-tossed waves,
Running wild and free

BUDGIE JUMPING

There was a full moon rising, Barry the budgie couldn't wait
if that hamster didn't go to sleep, it would make him late
He firtled in the seed tray, and pulled out a golden key
opened up the cage door, quietly, then he was out and free

He hopped across the carpet, unlocked the window latch
Glided across the garden, and out beyond the nettle patch
A host of elves and fairies waited for Barry there
with a shimmering golden harness, jewels everywhere

They painted his wings with rainbows, fastened reins and tack
Brought a set of tiny steps, then the elves climbed on his back
As he swept up to the treetops with a whooping group of elves
the fairies flew in arabesques, made bets among themselves

He reached the highest point, chirped, and tossed his head
and the elves leapt into nowhere, each tied to a silken thread,
With each glistening, fragile tether held tight in sturdy claws
they twirled, bounced, twisted, and screamed without a pause
The fairies flew in closer, encouraged them in their excess
Gave points for style and content, judged which elf was best
When he swooped back to the ground, for another cheering group,
they fed him grapes and raisins, and sips of sunflower soup

At last a mighty horn blew, and the elves all groaned as one
It had hardly seemed a moment, but now the night was gone
So they removed his golden harness, unclipped the silken threads
As the dawn burst into life, he flapped wearily home to bed

Barry hopped back to his cage, washed the colours from his wings
Locked the door, hid the key, went to sleep up on his swing
Thereafter 'pretty boy', sent his thoughts drifting away
to moonlit nights, on rainbow wings, budgie jumping with the fey

BUILT WITH LOVE

I have tried to build this bridge
using all that I can find
Used every memory of you,
from every corner of my mind
Neither of us on our own
can reach the other side
But only you will ever know
how very hard I've tried
For I have anchored it
with all the love I ever felt for you
Knowing that you'll anchor your side
just as tight and just as true

So when this bridge is finished,
on the day you hear my call
Cross straight over, do not hesitate,
it cannot let you fall
And the moment that you cross,
and once more we are together
This aching void will disappear,
completely, and for ever

BYE, POLAR

Under flaming Northern skies
Lord of this frozen paradise
Onward with unchanging pace
Across the endless icy waste

Daylight after months of dark
Listening for the first seal bark
More urgent now with every day
Relentless search, dwindling prey

All too soon the time of floes
Cautious, stalking warier foes
Then endless seas, endless sky
Summer, too slow, slipping by

Unknowing, anticipates the snows
To recreate the land he knows
Famine sapping strength and life
Searching now for Polar wife

Though he searches everywhere
No Polar Queen his seed will bear
All too soon, 'neath blazing sun
The final Polar Bear is - gone

A CATHOLIC EDUCATION

(Check definitions of catholic before throwing bibles)

Dancing naked, a vision of heaven
Uncle Bill liked that, when she was just seven

Blokes put their hands down her pants, but then
The priest first did that when she was ten

The first time it hurt, and then it was sore
By twelve she felt nothing much there any more

She thought it unpleasant, not really obscene
Tried not to swallow, gave up at thirteen

She did it for money, she wasn't that keen
It paid Mum's debts, she was only fourteen

She was just a girl with a catholic upbringing
Began education while choirs were singing
Continued by teachers, family and vicars
with versatile ways to get into her knickers
She learned that penance would be on her knees
Absolution coming from those she pleased
Until lawyers and judges all called it a crime
Inflicted fines, and then gave her time
Where her education continued apace
and she found it all felt better when spaced
Couldn't feed the growing addiction, so then
She used dirty needles and dirtier men
Infected, neglected, starved and abused
Her short brutal span was soon all used
Let's pray she found, when her body was cold
The One who loved her just for her soul

CONCRETED IMPRESSIONS

I paused by a grate in the street one day
and above the traffic's hum
Heard the ghost of water shaping stone
where once a stream had run

Saw the flash of sun on silver scales
Saw the glint of a kingfisher's wing
Heard the babble of sparkling shallows
Heard the cuckoo and nightingale sing
Smelled roses and honeysuckle
and, oh, the scent of meadows in spring!

Remembered when my world was young
Felt a smile I thought was gone
Wood smoke tickled in my nose
My arm itched from the rambling rose
That bumbling puppy who grew so fast
Dusk, a badger snuffling past ......

Then something big grated it's gears
I think it was a bus
The usual cacophony crashed back in
and Paradise was - lost

CROCODILE WOOD

Yesterday, I went out for a walk
with Scooby, to Crocodile Wood
At first I couldn't see Crocodiles
but I squinted, and then I could!

It's a good job Jonathan warned me
or we might have walked too near
Jonathan says they are lazy
if we're quiet, there's nothing to fear

I was careful where I put my feet
Ratty and Mole are quite small
and putting my foot through Flopsy's door?
Well, that wouldn't do at all

We both were very keen to meet
Mouse or The Gruffalo
or Ephalump, Teddy and Batty Bat
I wondered, where did they go?

Then I saw both Owl and Squirrel
up high, in the top of a tree
and realise, because I'm grown up
they don't want to play with me

CRYING COUNTRY

It's the end of another long, lost and lonely day
I've run right out of curses, I've forgotten how to pray
Whispering Bob comes on the radio, country guitars play
and I've got no more troubles,
'cos my tears just washed them away

I don't have much luck with loving, if I do it goes astray
My romantic history reads like a country song or Shakespeare play
So I play that country music, when she tells me she can't stay
no scars upon my heart,
'cos the tears have washed them away

The aching memories and joints, age bites in so many ways
It could be a misspent youth, or a life of work and not much play
But country music soothes me, relaxing at the close of day
no more pains or sorrows,
'cos the tears just wash them away

Country songs sing sad tales, of broken hearts and dreams
They sing the story of my life, at least that's how it seems
So after each disaster, I just let that music play
and the scars and memories fade,
'cos the tears just wash it all away

This poor old world is now a dirty, dark and ugly place
with our bodies full of poison, and the fear upon every face
When I can't take it any more, I let that country music play
and my world is fresh and bright,
'cos the tears wash it all away

I have always been a sinner, and damnation should be my fate
The preacher won't give salvation, and remorse would be too late
So I'll play that country music, and you'll see on Judgement Day
no stains upon my soul,
'cos my tears will have washed them away

DANCE ETERNAL

Forever on the sands of time
Your footprints always next to mine
Side by side, on eternity's floor
In perfect step for evermore
Unseen, unheard, yet always there
Close beside me everywhere
In perfect step, in perfect rhyme
Their cadence beating perfect time

Side by side, heel and toe
To the unheard rhythm of life they flow
Soft and slow, leap and prance
That pulse dictates each step we dance
Together forever, we will dance on
Hearts beating to that eternal drum
Inseparable 'til the end of time
Hearts and footsteps, a perfect rhyme

DESOLATE

In the endless burning wastes
where only silence speaks
Up above the snow line
where lost souls roam the peaks
Entombed in vaulted caverns
a mountain, eternal, weeps
There, lost in desolation
my grieving soul it's vigil keeps

In the heart of roiling thunderheads
where angels dare not fly
Where raucous flocks of ravens swoop
their cowering prey to scry
Beneath the crimson shadows
of this torn and bleeding sky
Souls of the lost and broken come
Drawn by my tortured spirit's cry

DIERDRE
THE FAIRY BLACKSMITH

60 verses and growing ....

Dierdre the fairy blacksmith was having a proper sulk
She had the will, a bit of skill, but totally lacked the bulk
No problem for the Ogres, muscles through and through
Dierdre was a fairy, she was petite, and girly too

All the smiths were Ogres, which she thought most unfair
No smithy code forbade dresses, or having lots of hair
The trouble was that iron stuff is big and very heavy too
Dierdre had trouble with her nails, never mind a whole horseshoe

Dierdre trained and sweated, not a really good look for a fae
But she couldn't build the muscle, she just wasn't made that way
and as for mending shields or swords, or armour on a stand
Dierdre couldn't sharpen daggers, unless somebody lent a hand

Soon she was totally frustrated by the attributes she lacked
Her hair was knotted and sooty, her nails were chipped and cracked
So Dierdre went to see her Dad, an extremely crafty elf
So sneaky everyone called him Sly - when he was only twelve

He gave her a Phoenix feather, plucked by the light of the moon
bound with hair from a Unicorn's mane, tied by a blind Baboon
Dierdre just sat and snivelled, "Very funny, Dad" she said
"I need help with my ambition, I get a silly feather instead"

But Dad insisted she tried it, and Dierdre, surprised and pleased
found that iron, lightly feathered, could be thrown around with ease
Dierdre was filled with excitement, her talent was all ablaze
Her plans for ferric construction would keep the kingdom amazed

The trouble was that Sly made the feather, his reputation was grim
Although the output was perfect, she wondered just what he put in
It was just such an annoyance, in the end she had to ask
"Dad, I'm pleased with the feather, how did you accomplish the task?"

"The Phoenix bit is fireproof, that takes care of the forging part
and moonlight lifts the lowest spirit, lightens the heaviest heart
Baboons can tie knots in anything, but a blind one can't tell what
I gave him a ticket to Africa, you can't be much fairer than that

and Unicorns only like maidens, that's what the mane is about
If some cheeky blighter nicks it, he'll go crackers working it out"
She said she was sorry for doubting, said she had been unfair
He told her to sort out her wardrobe, and fix up her nails and hair

She had to be careful with dresses, silk and taffeta soon were alight
The Dierdre look developed - Asbestos and leather, cheerful and bright
Her wings she kept tightly closed, protected and tucked out of sight
Wings of fire look really gorgeous, but they're not any good for flight

Dierdre fired up her furnace, played heavy metal in excess
Made helmets, swords and cooking pots, lingerie for a young Trolless
But although her wares were amazing, light and extremely strong
Nobody ever bought them, she couldn't work out what was wrong

Then a passing Gnomish trader, in a startling fit of unpaid pity
Said no-one believed her stuff was real, didn't trust a fairy smithy
With birdsong, flowers and murals, the ambience was askew
No smoke, no sparks, no swearing, no smells to make you say "Phew"

Poor Dierdre was so downhearted, she sat down for a real good cry
She was heard by a spotty young squire, who was miserably trudging by
His training came to her rescue, 'A Maiden - and in such distress!'
He gave sympathy and a hanky, you can't mop with an asbestos dress

So he told her his many troubles, while Dierdre bemoaned her fate
Soon they felt a great deal better, but he had to go, it was late
He told her his name was Kevin, "Dierdre" she shyly replied
He promised to purchase on payday, but she thought he probably lied

But Friday week on the dot, Kevin turned up clutching his pay
Tried to find something he could afford, just to make her day
She brought out her finest weaponry, swore all the work was hers
With a sudden thrill she realised, he wanted her and not her wares!

Dierdre was chaste, and Kevin was chasing, but didn't know what to do
Kevin had heard all the ballads, love was noble, gentle and true
Dierdre had heard the fairy songs, where love was exciting and rough
But neither one was experienced, so they both were relying on bluff

Then eventually, in desperation, Kevin blurted out in fright
"I'd love to buy a horseshoe, but I'd rather buy you dinner tonight
There's a lovely place I've heard of, you may know it, Dragon Spit
The new chef there is really good, I wondered if you fancy it"

She had heard of it all right, Dad had warned her about the place
But Dierdre quickly agreed to go, with a modest blush on her face
On the night she dressed up properly, with a frock and frilly stuff
so she wouldn't be embarrassed if it went well and things got rough

Kevin had a proper bath, and wore his best doublet and hose
Dierdre tried not giggle, when she saw him arriving in those
He opened the door and offered his hand, trying hard to be posh
It didn't really matter to Dierdre, she knew that he had no dosh

A Gremlin came in with a snarl on her face, and her miniskirt askew
"The chef won't be coming back" she said, "so its Dragonburger or Stew"
There are questions you shouldn't ask, you may hate the answer you get
So they ordered two portions of Stew, and hoped it was no-one's pet

Dierdre said the Stew was nice, but not what it might be nice for
Then the Gremlin came ambling over, with a hatchet clutched in her paw
"You're that fairy blacksmith, with the forge that's all squeaky clean
I keep blunting this on Dragon bone, can you fix it so it stays keen?"

Delighted by the commission Dierdre whooped her acceptance with glee
Then realised she had no feather, and how heavy the hatchet must be
There was no way Dierdre could lift it, she was going to look so effete
But Kevin offered to carry it, which she thought was foolish, but sweet

She boasted when she had fixed it, "this will now do so much more.
Nothing is harder than Gremlin nails, but with this you can manicure"
Next time she called, upon the wall was a satyr's head on a hook
"Since you fixed my hatchet" Gremlin grinned, "I get no hassle from cook"

Dierdre kept the Gremlin's payment, the very first shekel she'd earned
She didn't really need any money, but Kevin did, she quickly learned
He would never be able to graduate, claim a coat of arms and spurs
Unless he won a tournament, but a horse, and all the kit, came first

Dierdre said not to worry, her weapons and armour would stop all attacks
Kevin wanted to pay, but Sly said that she could set it off against tax
As advertising of her wares since when the spotty young erk was beat
When they wiped off all the blood, his armour would be pristine and neat

Dierdre daren't tell Kevin, she was determined her man would win
She built him a suit of armour that was supertough and as light as tin
Now all they needed was a steed, but winced when told the cost
The only nags that were cheaper, were rejects, lame, or had lost

On the day of the sale of reject steeds, four groats was all Kevin had
But Dierdre had her Gremlin's shekel, she said "its not that bad"
They went off to the market, hopefully clutching the groats and shekel
"You bargain with him", Dierdre said, "while I stand over here and heckle"

So Kev asked "why call it Booty, when it looks much more like a goat?"
"Because that's what was written on the bag that came with his oats"
Poor Booty was a scruffy brown horse, not tall, and not very strong
But Kevin paid out a bit too much, just to get him away from the pong

Dierdre was quite put out, Kevin smiled and took hold of her hand
"He really likes me", he said, "and I knew a Fairy would understand"
Dierdre couldn't resist that smile, and admitted she did like horses
Didn't mention she'd rather have hers on a spit with barbeque sauces

They finally got their Booty home, though they had to help in places
Thought they should feed him up before putting him through his paces
He certainly had an appetite, Dierdre had to appeal to the fae
Who let her raid the their stash of apples and dried wild oats in hay

He quickly put on lots of weight, only some of which was muscle
but Kevin said he still was too weak to carry armour and tussle
Dierdre reminded him that even her armour for horses was very light
So they bought the local papers, and started looking for a fight

They had to wait 'til next payday, the entrance fee was half a crown
Kevin said it was worth it, he was going to win her the May Queen's crown
It went to the champion at the end, when all the contests were finished
The one who beat the rest, whose fighting record was totally unblemished

Sly looked at the competition rules, and what Kevin could realistically manage
He bet everything he could borrow on Kevin surviving totally undamaged
Sly didn't rate Kev's fighting skills, thought he'd be smashed into the dirt
But he had faith in his oddball daughter, Kevin would lose, but wouldn't get hurt

The odds against Kevin were so great the bookie's thought that Sly was a nutter
Dierdre had a sixpence, she bet on a win, because most Fairies like a flutter
When she saw her beau's opponent, a metal mountain carrying a banner
The Knight in his full metal jacket was enough to make her fear for her tanner

"Hurry up, Sir Basilisk" screamed, "I'm going to flatten this blaggard"
When his armoured bulk hit the saddle, his poor horse actually staggered
Off plodded two tons of armour with only a ton of horse inside
It developed a list all of its own if he held out his lance out to the side

With slimline lightweight armour, Booty looked like a schoolgirl's pet
Sir Basilisk started chuckling, this would be the easiest victory yet
Rider and horse were wearing suits as thin as baked bean cans
the horse was prancing and twirling, Kevin even had a lightweight lance

You were only allowed two charges, to prove you were the best
the horse was worn out then, and usually needed two days rest
But Sir Basilisk was certain, one run would be more than enough
The slightest tap on his armour, and Kevin would just be mush

He aimed his lance at Kevin and then carefully lined up his horse
once all that weight was moving, you couldn't alter your course
Kevin was much more cavalier, hardly seemed to aim at all
The lad was an obvious amateur, and was heading for a very hard fall

Dierdre was too scared to look, found a mug to hide behind
Most mugs were betting on how many pieces of Kevin they'd find
Kevin came racing back into view, at tremendous velocity
She flew a triumphant loop the loop, squealed in very unladylike glee

Sir Basilisk was totally baffled, this was not like a proper fight
Just before his lance hit Kevin, Booty dodged to the right
He had never missed his target, not since he was just turned ten
and he was riding the dog and trying to skewer the cat back then

His charger, puffing and panting, pretended that he felt fine
while Booty practised prancing, out in front of the filly line
Sir Basilisk was focussed, his record of wins in danger
and he'd bet a fortune on victory against this spotty stranger

Again they hurled across the turf, the crowd was silenced now
Could Kevin and Booty survive a second time, and if so, how
Dierdre watched aghast, as the juggernaut thundered down
then Kevin dipped his lance, and knocked the other towards the ground!

Booty swerved nimbly aside again, and then Basilisk's lance bit the dirt
You've probably seen the pole vault, well in armour it really hurts
His horse looked fairly happy, after all it was done for the day
Some trolls painted with crosses came and dragged the knight away

Booty and Kevin had triumphed, so they pranced around for a bit
They were ready to have another go, after all they hadn't been hit
But the rules said Booty was tired, and couldn't take the chance
So they retired to Kevin's tent, where Dierdre notched his lance

Steeds are smarter than riders, who are often concussed by a whack
They could see how easily Booty had avoided each lunge and attack
They showed bottoms to the grooms, stuck their heads into their oats
Clearly they were all on strike, for Dierdre's lighweight armoured coats

Kevin had won the jousting, since nobody else's warhorse would fight
Dierdre wanted to celebrate, Kevin was shy, said he had to sleep tonight
The following morning Dierdre wondered if she'd missed her chance of fun
because Kevin wouldn't be dodging on foot, he could only fight or run

Sir Basilisk had recovered enough to re-appear with revenge in mind
equipped to bash and chop and stab, and to generally be very unkind
The other knights were curious, and happy Basilisk wanted first go
If Kevin had a sneaky trick, he'd use it on Bas, and then they'd know

The only trick that the young squire had, was to run far away, very fast
his armour made it easy, the crowd were wondering how long he could last
If lightweight Kevin could keep it up, dodge a fight for long enough
Sir Basilisk might just fall over, within minutes he'd run right out of puff

Unfortunately the crowd were bored, they wanted a fight, not a day at the races
They threw soggy sprouts and squash, booed and pulled unpleasant faces
The umpire said the crowd had paid, they wanted blood, it was their right
Kevin would forfeit the contest if he didn't stop prancing and turn and fight.

Sir Basilisk's sword came whistling round, aimed straight at Kevin's head
They expected him to dodge again, he brought up his shield instead
Crash! The sword connected, with an ear-splitting screech and bang
The birds all fluttered off squawking, while the pigs and dogs just ran

The resulting vibrations spread out, and back up Sir Basilisk's arm
He felt them invade his chest and legs, and his eyes went wide in alarm
They reached his feet and he juddered off in a circle around everyone
'til he caught his heel on a rock, and went crashing down onto his bum

When he rose they thought he'd be livid, but he dropped his sword instead
For a knight, embarrassment is worse than a great big bash on the head
What finished him off was an ancient Gnome, perched on the Umpire's hat
Who was pointing and laughing hysterically, Sir Basilisk couldn't face that

The other knights and men-at-arms conferred, (they usually fought)
Instead of bashing and battering, they were shocked into trying thought
None of them were worried much about bleeding, concussion or death
But not a single one would risk becoming the object of Gnomish mirth

As nobody else would fight the lad, the judges were left with very few choices
They had to give Kevin the victory, despite the many dissenting voices
Against all the odds, and there were a lot, Kevin the squire was a Knight
He was now the May Day champion, unbeaten, the prize was his by right

He offered the coveted crown to Dierdre, causing her great distress
She had only come to help him out, and was wearing her smithying dress!
But her Mum came zipping through the crowd, looked Dierdre up and down
Nicked lace and ribbons from some hats, and whipped up a fabulous gown

Dierdre feathered the heavy crown and held it high for all to admire
She sat on his helm and smiled and waved, until at last they could retire
Keven was hyped and forgot to be shy, when she fluttered down for a kiss
So she gave him an eyeful of undies, and finally managed a glimpse of his

Then he went all bashful and masterful, the combination was appealing
Kevin swore undying love, and admitted some very unknightly feelings
The Lord threw a truly wild party, where they all agreed Kevin was lucky
except Sly, who left with his winnings, before he was caught by the bookie

Dierdre sold out of everything, even the codpiece shaped like a bream
Customers, and a Knight at night, she fulfilled every one of her dreams
The Ogre smiths were very upset, predicted Dierdre's imminent fall
The Gremlin put the word out, she had empty hooks on the café wall

The local ladies of the night found they could advertise their charms
and if someone got enthusiastic, steel lace kept them safe from harm
Sometimes even a Dragoness, with a slightly embarrassed blush
would purchase caps for broken claws, or a filigreed sheath for a tusk

The snobbiest ladies couldn't deny that Dierdre's wares had appeal
That season many a decolletage showed the modest gleam of steel
At last the wife of Sir Basilisk completed our Dierdre's redemption
had a lovely chat with her, discussed controlling metallic vibration

DIESEL AND COW

The cars had all pulled over
up and down our village street
A tractor slowly trundled past
Small and old, but clean and neat

I thought that's very nice and shrugged
but here came another, nearly the same
Then a gap, then a slightly larger one
and another, then a small one again

I stood and watched, open mouthed
memory lane had taken me
I was losing the plot at eleven o'clock
when I usually last until three

One after the other, bright and proud
in reds and yellows, greens and blues
They look so small against modern ones
but that only seems strange to you

Washed and painted, polished and primped
as they sometimes do with Shires
There were Masseys, Nuffields, Harvesters
A John Deere with one front tyre

I rushed outside to drink it up
to catch them before they were gone
It's strange how the smell of diesel and cow
brings life back to these old bones

Not horses, they don't want treat
Tho' one chap used to work with his cat
in the box, for friends, behind the seat
No modern gadget has perks like that

I'll never know the reason
Where they went or from whence they came
But I look outside, hopeful, each Sunday
just in case they come back again

DISCO LEN

Len should have been out on the town
doing hamster this and that
But he was much too frightened
of the neighbour's pussy cat
It tried to pounce on him from nowhere
but sometimes, worst of all
It sneaked in through the door
and chased him up and down the hall

But Marion, his mummy
was looking out for her wee chap
She would chase that pussy out again
would hiss and sometimes clap
Len couldn't carry on like this
he became a bag of nerves
He dreamt of being tough
of giving puss what he deserved

Then one day Marion bought a ball
for him, so he could play
He wanted to, didn't know how
so Mum showed him the way
She rolled around the floor
he caught on in nothing flat
and then he realised, inside
Len was safe from the pussy cat

So he rolled around the floor each night
when his mummy called
Then he realised he got stronger
the more he used that ball
Len rolled it up and down
and back and forth he went as well
The more he rolled his ball
well, the more his muscles swelled

The cat still caught him sometimes
knocked his ball about
But Len persisted, waiting
until he knew the time was right
The cat hissed, jumped on his ball
gave it a fearsome whack
Len climbed out, smoothed his fur
and then he hissed right back

He dished out two big uppercuts
gave that cat an awful fright
Then ninja kicked it down the hall
and it streaked off, out of sight
Now Len is a confident hamster
he's the funkiest of them all
and he's always out on Saturday nights
rolling his disco ball !!

DO NOT BUG US

That Spider, don't deride her
you must have grown up in a city
They need eight legs to spin their webs
and make the hedges pretty

Don't flick sticks at Water Boatmen
they can't handle the abuse
They hurtle around in circles
become totally confused

Keep your flagstones clean and tidy
for slimy Slugs and Snails
They cannot travel through the gravel
it obliterates their trails

Flinging seeds into the reeds
gives the Dragonflies a fright
They cause bother to each other
by reversing in mid-flight

Pinging peas at Bumblebees
is not the smartest thing
They have a temper, and remember
Bumblebees can sting

Butterflies dislike french fries
they just won't hang around
So keep your chips between your lips
not scattered on the ground

We Faeries need these tiny steeds
in the jungle you call garden
Causing commotion in our locomotion
- this we cannot pardon

DOES SHE THINK OF ME

Is she walking down the hillside
as the sun sinks in the sea
Is she sitting watching ships go by
and does she think of me?
Is she laid out making angels
in the freshly fallen snow
Making funny froggie footprints
with her cheeks and eyes aglow

Digging pools, or damming
some stream across a beach
Hanging over cliff tops
for the flowers she cannot reach
Chasing dogs and seagulls
in the early morning mist
Walking in the sunshine
her nose and cheeks sun-kissed

Is she sitting by the fire
drinking chocolate in the glow
Wondering when I'm coming
and why she had to go
I would love to go and join her
see her eyes go warm and bright
How I wish I had the courage
to step into endless night

DOGS OF WAR

Across the blood-soaked killing fields
through the shattered streets,
Comes the rumble of their iron wheels
a thousand marching feet
The Dogs of War have come
to buy your freedom with their lives
To spend all their tomorrows
for your children and your wives

Down in the ruined cellars
where the children crouch in fear
Comes a whisper of salvation
and the shadow of a cheer
Through the hallways of oppression
comes a shadow and a chill
The Dogs of War are hunting
they are closing for the kill

Cheer them as they march away
(but curses from your wives)
Your child is marching too
replacing those who gave their lives
They have no god or country
they will win, or they will fall
Always marching into battle
bringing peace or death to all

DOUR

Dour grey empty sky, o'er dour grey empty street
Nae early morning babble, nae clatter o' booted feet
Nae pitter patter skippin, nae lads out kickin 't can
Nae fish, nae yards, nae factories - it's nae life forra man

DRACONIAN NURTURE

A rustle and a puff of smoke
as something tiny breathes
Under a bush, a dragonet
curled up in the leaves
He chirped, sounded hungry
and tried very hard to stand
He was obviously deserted
He fitted nicely in my hand

I made him up a little bed
it caught fire quite a lot
So after that he always slept
in my best cooking pot
I fed him milk and buttered toast
stroked his tiny head
With practice he stopped smoking
and produced a flame instead

He rode upon my shoulder
but was naturally shy
Would duck under my collar
if somebody passed close by
He started flapping with his wings
just practising at first
Then one day really opened them
a glorious crimson burst

Once he could fly a little bit
he went on walks with me
The lead went up not sideways
a peculiar sight to see
We had to be quite cautious
you know how funny people are
I wanted him up in the clouds
not pickled in a jar

In the autumn we collected fruit
and nuts from all around
Without his lead, he flew so high
but always came back down
I'd hear the tinkle of his bell
high up in the tree
First he'd roast a chestnut
then he'd throw it down for me

We knew this wouldn't last for ever
knew this bliss must end
That he needed to find dragons
to be wild, not just my friend
So I took him to the seaside
to the cliffs and golden sands
He chirped a little, spread his wings
flew up, out of my hands

He checks up on me now and then
always late at night
I see a gleam of crimson wing
his jewelled eyes, so bright
He's grown up now and moved away
I'd love to see him more
But he still leaves tiny heaps
of roasted chestnuts by my door

THE DRAGON HUNTERS

In spring I love to sit and watch
the dragons as they play
But I can't find one anywhere
although I searched all day
I put the toast and milk out
on the windowsill last night
It was there, untouched, this morning,
something isn't right

Then in the fields I see
the dragon hunters with their prey
They trap them, and cage them
they take them far away
Folk who live in distant cities,
sterile piles of heartless stone
Like to keep a little wilderness
imprisoned in their homes

Those who purchase dragons
have been cheated in the end
Dragons are wild, free spirits,
they will never be your friend
They pine and fade in cages
dream of open fields and sky
Scales and eyes grow dull
and have you heard a dragon cry?

In those places dragon hunters went
to ply their cruel trade
Some spark is missing now
as the magic starts to fade
Folk are much too slow to laugh,
see how easily they cry
Without that glorious lift of spirit
when a dragon passes by

When the dragon hunters leave,
take our fiery friends away
They'll take the magic from our lives,
I cannot live that way
Tonight all of my friends
are coming to the camp with me
To smash the locks and traps
and set all the dragons free !!

THE DRAGON OF AUTUMN

Last night the wind was rising
it seemed the perfect sign
I settled down to watch
determined not to doze this time
But sleep stole gently through me
Dreams held me entranced
The magic moment passed
and once more I missed my chance

During the night, unseen
breathing magic over the world
The Dragon of Autumn passed
and now his spell's unfurled
As it touched the fruit and berries
they ripen in his wake
Pass a message to each creature
of wood, or field or lake

Touched each leaf and stained it
left a spark that slowly grew
Until, clouds of clumsy butterflies
they left the trees, and flew
Painting every nook and cranny
drifting as they flutter down
Footpaths becoming rainbows
Kaleidoscopes, being reblown

Passing through my orchard
he blessed every bush and tree
The rosy glow on every apple
dragon kisses, it seems to me
Each hip and haw, each blackberry
presents to save until,
Each a drop of summer
they bring warmth to winter's chill

The evergreens stand proud
untouched, still glowing green
Immune to dragon magic
each coated with protective sheen
Giving warmth and shelter
to keep the frost and snow at bay
Safe for bugs and birds
and hedgehogs sleeping winter away

As the message passes
watch how everyone prepares
Gathering food and bedding
stores to serve as winter fare
Building strength for awesome flights
to flee the arctic blast
To wait in distant, sun-baked exile
until our winter's past

I can feel the echo of his flight
coursing through my veins
I still receive the message
but man's spirit has been tamed
But it's not too long, if I am patient
the magic is not lost
The Dragon of Spring is coming soon
to blow away the frost

DRAGONHEART

The secret of dragons, of how they are made
is to find one perfect, pure piece of Jade
Be sure it is clear, with no fracture or stain
a flaw in it's heart will be your dragon's bane
Because this is the secret, this is the start
from this you can grow a true dragon's heart.

Polish it gently, use velvet gloves
Steep it in loyalty, soak it in love
Bathe it in happiness, splash it with fun
Sprinkle with laughter until it is done
When the magic awakes, with a soft gentle glow
This is your seed, now your dragon can grow!
Take care how you treat it, this is no toy,
if you treat it too roughly, you may get a boy!
Find a place, both secret and safe,
never doubt, always keep your faith
Gather ingredients, with exquisite care
Then once you are ready, take the seed there

You will need two Opals, these will be eyes
so she can look both mysterious and wise
Ivory, for the fangs she must grow
polished to bring out that lustrous glow
Diamond chips for claws so keen
that will never need sharpening, always stay clean
Stainless steel pins in various lengths
for bones, to give them extra strength
Silver bells so she speaks in song
a little granite, for when life goes wrong
Jet and Mother of Pearl for her scales
patterned and shaded from nose to tails
and to set off all those wondrous things
Lapis lazuli for her wings

Pile all of these treasures over the seed
as it grows, it will need them to feed
Tend it alone, there can be only one
do not neglect it, once you've begun
Protect it from magpies, squirrels and such
don't expose it to rain too much
Uncover it often to soft moonlight
the starry depths of a clear, still night
Caress it with the dawning sun
toughen it with a frost, just one
Garland it with the first spring flowers
nurture it in your secret bower

Don't be upset, despite the surprise
all new-born dragons start that size
Bring her insects, find her worms
don't feed by hand, dragon breathe burns!
Although she is only as big as a mouse
in a hundred years she'll be hunting cows
Dragons keep growing, no-one knows why
and from the very first day, she will fly!
Teach her caution, teach her stealth
that scientists are bad for her health
She will look to you, always be there
encourage good manners, show her you care
Don't fear getting old, you'll never part
your spirit will fly to the dragon's heart

When she grows too big for earthly skies,
up to the stars your dragon flies
She will roam the universe far from earth
but always remember the place of her birth
and one day fly home, no matter how far
So when you see a shooting star
it may just be a dragon coming back home
To check what has happened, while they were gone
For wherever they roam, in their heart of Jade
They carry the spirit from whom they were made

Millennia from now, she will reach the size
where planets are blown aside where she flies
Then the fearsome flame in her magical heart
will grow, and consume her, every part
But the dragon lives on, and her magic flows
til warmth and life from cold stone grows
There's a dragon in our sky every morn
for this is the way a new star is born ....

DUNN'S BROWN COW

I know she's Welsh, but it makes no sense
Dunn's brown cow just jumped that fence!
I'm buying a camera because quite soon
If she keeps it up she'll jump the moon

They caught her and raised the stable door
she jumped that as well, was gone once more
No point searching the fields and the lanes
She'll be going for gold at the Commonwealth games

Now it's wild west time, out Kettleby way
they've built a corral, and filled it with hay
But the boys ride Friesian heifers of course
since a welsh brown cow outjumps a horse

Wildish cowboys with waterproof hoodies
and proper wellies, green and muddy
Though their roping skills aren't really the best
since the iLassoo won't clear up this mess

I'm marking mid-August in red for next year
and hoping to sell all my homemade beer
They're knitting tea-cosies with horns and a tail
and planting flowers in old kitchen pails

It's the Somerby rodeo, locals are thrilled
Already they've had several entrants from Rhyll
For the hurdles of course, I'm taking bets now
but my money's going on Dunn's brown cow

EARTHBOUND

If I had the wings of an angel
my feet would still be clay
Until I can set my spirit free
we can never fly away ....

I find that with my spirit free
it needs no wings to fly
Which leaves me still here on the ground
waving it goodbye

EDDIES FIREWORKS

"Will we have fireworks this year?"
Eddie asked his Mum
as he put out the dish of milk
and a little heap of crumbs
"No money love," she sadly said
"your Dad has lost his job
We'll try to get some sparklers,
we can find a couple of bob"

Next night as well as milk
he put out some buttered toast
whispered his dearest wish
(Granpa said they would be close)
When the magic night arrived
with nose on the window pane
Eddie watched distant rockets
his plea had been in vain

Then beyond their tiny bonfire
a flicker of silver flame
He concentrated on the spot
yes, there it was again!
Something shot into the night
at a hundred miles an hour
Exploded into flame above
a giant, multicoloured flower

And all along the fence
rainbow fountains spouted high
Sparks flowed like a waterfall
fireballs began to fly
Past the window, slowly
flew a catherine wheel so bright
and everywhere he looked
coloured flames lit up the night

"Wow, thank you Dad!" he shouted
but Dad was still inside
Standing open-mouthed,
sparklers, unlit, at his side
When Eddie looked again,
there, upon the windowsill
Was a tiny crimson dragon
drinking up the bowl of milk

It glided to the shed
wound its tail around the handle
and fired off a string of fireballs
a living Roman Candle
Now he could see that
there were dragons everywhere
Producing fiery treats
with tremendous skill and flair

Above the whoosh of flames
he could hear a pattering sound
as the children ran, enchanted
from the houses all around
First they watched the dragons playing
with just a little fear
Dragonets spread out among them
they all began to cheer

Then Mums and Dads arrived
each brought a little treat
An impromptu dragon barbecue
developed in the street
As the little dragons landed
exhausted, one by one
Each received a little bowl of milk
and a tiny toasted bun

But such excitement couldn't last
eyelids began to close
Little dragonets and children
one by one began to doze
Were carried off to bed
to dream their magic dreams
As the dragons flew away
tiny, fading, coloured gleams

Last, the crimson dragon
gave Eddie a farewell bark
Bounced, crackling, down the road
like an animated spark
No-one talks about it much
but the local windowsills
Each night bear buttered toast
and bowls of warm, fresh milk!

EDMUND
THE DANCING KANGAROO

Edmund the baby Kangaroo
thought he was a flop
He could walk around quite nicely
but he couldn't hop
He brought his left foot up
the right one stayed down there
No matter how he tried
they wouldn't function as a pair

His mother tried to help him
to develop hopping habits
His father did his best
bought him wallabies and rabbits
The kookaburra laughed
and said between his squawks
A tasty dingo dinner, mate
is a kangaroo that walks

One day salvation happened
he heard a rhythmic sound
and one by one his feet
started moving on the ground
One foot shuffled sideways
then gave a quick sharp tap
The other one did just the same
so he added in a clap

Before he knew it both his feet
became a blur of motion
Independent synchronicity
he was lost in the emotion
He'd never seen a kangaroo
who moved with such élan
They'd need to learn to walk
so he's the only one who can

He tried a small experiment
put steel tips on his claws
Stood on a stump and tapdanced
for hours without a pause
He spun and leapt and twirled
pirouetted left and right
He'd practise near the stockmen
because they sang at night

They used to laugh at him and jeer
but they remember still
When joking stopped
and suddenly they realised his skill
The fateful night they played him
a Michael Jackson song
and Edmund the Kangaroo
moonwalked around the billabong

They came for him with traps and nets
horses and lassoes
He was famous now from coast to coast
He made the evening news
But though they keep on looking
and I suppose they'll never stop
He now blends in with his cousins
'cos he taught himself hip-hop

He's still the only kangaroo
that can truly walk and dance
Still answers the call of music
whenever he gets the chance
Those nights some lucky stockman
enchanted, from afar
can watch Edmund the Kangaroo
merrily dance beneath the stars

EMOTIONAL OUTBURST

Emotional turmoil, welling up from deep within
Tightening breath, flushing skin
Bubbling, leaking through damp lashes, bright wet eyes
Snorting, sneezing, in surprise
Rising exclamation, overwhelming, triumphant, intense
Roaring up, stifling all coherence
Bursting, bellowing, from wide-stretched, gaping maw
Limbs a-tremble, twitching on the floor
Guffaw explodes, exuberant merriment, the true worth -
of a puppy, the epitome of mirth!

ENABLEMENT

When pain first stole my morning walk
crippled limb and mind
All I could think was what I'd lost
how fate was so unkind
Then like a sunbeam in my heart
cutting through the gloom
A spark became a beacon
and poetry began to bloom

So now I run to greet the dawn
I soar through endless skies
All the mysteries of time and space
revealed before my eyes
The pain that ate me up
made me so miserable and terse
Is now lost against the splendour
of the poetic universe

My words can paint a panorama
full of colour, fire and life
An antidote to realities
to our modern, soul-less strife
Lift spirits on clouds of laughter
light fires in your heart
Bring the strongest to their knees
or break a world apart

Paint spots dropped on canvas
seeds in a forest glade
Rewriting our conceptions
transforming feather into blade
Poetry spreads and merges
ever bringing a different hue
So open up your heart
and let it's magic flow right through

ENDLESS NIGHT

Your breathing, soft, beside me in the night
Catches, stops my heart with sudden fright
Frozen, I wait, sudden dread has seized my will
You breathe, and all my foolish fears are stilled

The experts all say terminal, the doctors all say soon
So I await that moment, when your breath does not resume
I lay beside you, listening, through the night so endless
Greet you, waking, with soft caress, and smile so careless

I see you growing weary of this endless fight
Behind the brittle smile, yearning for endless night
My craven heart quails, I cannot face that dawn
When I must face the endless days - alone

- for my Noeline

ETERNAL WEAVE

When you walk into the dark
smile at the very end
For you will live on, eternal
in the memories of friends
A part of their existence
one strand within their lives
As long as they persist
some part of you always survives

Each time you are kind
add something to their world
You will create a highlight
one tiny gleaming curl
But should you cause them sadness
maybe a little pain
It shows up as a scuff
or some fraying from the strain

Some affect us strongly
leave colours bright and clear
Others are more subtle
just a gentle shading, here
Children become intense
learning as they grow
Older folk get fainter
relaxing, preparing to let go

People who are dearest
get a whole strand of their own
Add taste and colour to our lives
long after they are gone
With comfort in our sorrow
and the experience they give
They smooth our onward path
for as long as we shall live

Everyone who ever lived
right back to the dawn of man
Strands in one eternal weave
passed on from hand to hand

FALLIBLE

I could wish you were a demon
that my deeds would bring no shame
But in the darkness of my soul
Love would be a pristine stain

I would hope you were an angel
but then if we should meet
You would see the truth of all I am
with my sins laid at your feet

The good will all become angels
The evil are demons they say
But there seems to be no place for us
The ones with souls of grey

FIRST HARVEST

reaping since the crack of dawn
swathes, cut through rippling corn

guns and gundogs in a huddle
rabbits running in the stubble

sheaves fit neatly into place
lines of sweat on dusty face

so many people, what a crowd
thresher, dusty, smelly, loud

chaff inside my pants and shirt
mustn't show my muscles hurt

ripened grain a river of gold
farmer's daughter, eyes so bold

laid exhausted, we are done
ploughman's lunch for everyone

my first sip of luke warm beer
harvest-time in Lincolnshire

FISHING WITH FERDINAND

When I was only little
we spent summers by the sea
Grandad was a fisherman
caught fresh fish for our tea
I went out with him sometimes
preparing bait and such
but when he took me fishing
we never caught as much
I asked him why, he stroked
his bony whistle on it's string
said, come back when you're older
I'll teach you everything

Years later I came back to him
to settle down for life
To become a proper fisherman
with a cottage, and a wife
Soon after Grandad took me out
very early, on our own
Out of sight of land we stopped
and he let the anchor down
Into some tiny thimbles
he poured warm milk, from a flask
Spread out grapes, nuts and grain
a very strange repast

He blew his special whistle
and I saw the wavetops blur
Swooping, shining brightly
there were dragons everywhere!
In their claws each dragon
firmly held a wriggly fish
Grandpa stood up in the boat
and waved a silver dish
Put it gently on the table
and moved back a little way
Said sit quietly now and watch
don't frighten them away

One by one, into the hold
they dropped their fishy catch
Chose their favourite morsel
and perched upon the hatch
Blew little flames to toast them
careful not to burn their feet
Then spread their wings like rainbows
and ate their tiny treats
Mummy dragons with their dragonets
clinging to their scales
Gave each a thimble full of milk
quietening their wails

A beautiful crimson dragon
the size of a household cat
Landed, picked up the plate
and hopped onto Granpa's lap
He chirped and whistled quietly
toasted his slice of bread
Neatly finished every crumb
while the old man stroked his head
He said, Ferdinand's our dragon
the one I wanted you to meet
They all do what he tells them
so don't ever forget his treat

Grandad gave up fishing
stayed at home, but not for long
I think his soul flew out to sea
to join the dragon's song
Ferdinand still rules his world
but now I'm old and gray
I intend to take my grandson out
to meet my friend today
Time to give up fishing
I know what I'll miss the most -
Sitting quietly watching dragons play
and sharing dragon toast

FLYIN AMBER

One spark of life, it's brief fierce ecstasy
now sacrificed to greed
Overwhelmed, ensnared and erased
by the relentless blood of trees

As slow ages pass, the hills grow old
and rot sets amber free
For a brief wild blur of years
plaything of wind, rain and gravity

One last golden echo, then seized
in torrents liquid clasp
Swept away, never again to feel the sun
only rivers rocky rasp

To fall, unending, into the dark oblivion
of ocean's salted tomb
Crushed by aeons of unyielding weight
stamped into the heart of stone

The hand of time sprinkles oblivion
over the works of beast and man
But there, one frozen fragment
testament to life, where it all began

While legends of empires fade
and steel returns once more to rust
One timeless jewel sparkles
with the glories of millennia turned to dust

FLYING HOME

Through confusion, through disaster
though our worlds are torn apart
I will find my way to you, my love
by just following my heart

As a pigeon to the loft
or a magnet to the pole
My heart will fly to your heart
so once more it can be whole

FROZEN EVOLUTION

"How do you know your fridge has an elephant inside?"
They say "footprints in the butter, are something it can't hide."
They laugh, it's just a joke you see, but I'm not laughing now
Strange tracks in my paté make me wonder what? and how?

I thought of ants and spiders, but these tracks have toes, and claws
So I looked in all the corners, found the marks of tiny paws
There, at the end of them, behind the yoghurt pots
A tiny spiky creature, a living cartoon of Jack Frost

He said you've caught me now and I'm really quite impressed
But there's something you should hear before you call the press,
We used to paint with frost, upon your windows and the lakes
and you humans were enchanted by the wonders we'd create

But you stopped believing in us, so no food was left at night
and we all were slowly starving, in a truly desperate plight
We had an offer from the fridgemen, it sounded pretty good
We'd magic on and off a light, they'd give us homes and food
So the first thing you should do, if you lose your little light
Check if something spoiled, or you sealed the food tubs tight
We need feeding to work magic, if we're hungry we may leave
So when the engineer comes, he'll have a pixie up his sleeve
I became a little careless 'cos I know your eyes aren't good
But they'll sack me if you tell them I've been trekking through the food
I'm too old to go back to the wild, back to the begging bowl
Though I'd love to paint with frost again, it's the artist in my soul

Now when I raid the fridge for something munchy for myself
I remember my frost pixie, and leave a little on the shelf
And in the winter when it's frosty, I think its rather cool
He paints 'thank you' in patterns on the windows, and the pool

GYPSY HEART

I told her my heart must always fly
an albatross on the wind
But she paid no heed, in thought or need
and now is much more than a friend

So I fled to the distant mountains
and I sailed the the wide, wild seas
For a woman like her is too much of a woman
for gypsy boys like me

HARRIET THE HORNET

Harriet the Hornet couldn't underztand the fuzz
It zzeemed zzo right to her, to zzing inztead of buzz
But mum told Harriet, it juzt izzn't right and proper
for a pretty hornet girl, to be zzinging for her zzupper

No buzzing round the boyz, she found it much more fun
Zzinging in zzpring showerz, or zzerenading zzummer zzun
Zzpent hourz reziting zzonnets to flowerz and the treez
or compozing zztunning zzonataz for butterflyz and beez

The boyz would bully beezzz, but Harriet zzpent her time
winging zzinging through the zzky, or practizing a rhyme
Zhe didn't want to frighten people. with her vizious zztinger
If zhe had to be notoriouz, it zzhould be az a zzinger

Harriet went to Glaztonbury, thought it loud but entertaining
Tried a muzical, found the zzound of moozic zzo exzilarating
Went to zzingalongz with zzkylarkz, zzerenaded zzparrowz
As the Zztinging Zzinger, gave free performanzes in parkz

At lazt a zzcout dizcovered her diztinctive zztripez and zztyle
Zzaid he could make her famouz, and make himzelf a pile
Zzhe pozed for papperatzi, became a One Zzhow guezt
The critcz were in ecztacy, proclaimed zhe waz the bezt

Her Zzchoolteacherz gave interviewz, zaid zhe alwayz waz a trier
Zhe gave conzertz everywhere, became a very frequent flier
Harriet made an album, it zzoomed zztraight to number one
and to top it all her mother came on-zztage to zzing-along

HAUNTED GLADES

Dust gathers in the passageways
and tattered cobwebs festoon the vaulted halls
Earthworks and entrances overthrown
the innermost chambers laid open to the sky
This ancient steading, ancestral home
to bloodlines older than royal lineage claim
Now broken, all slain and scattered
in one night of treachery, blood and gunfire

No crime, no insult or injury brought this doom
this fell and dreadful fate
Babes slain at breast, mothers as they flee
the patter of young feet silenced
Yet who committed this crime
in whose name were families put to blade?
Why our name, by our elected servants
it is our hand that is stained for ever

These woods are silent now, roots writhe deep
grasses sprout on crumbling walls,
Fading from the memory of man.
Now mice winter in the dried wreckage of bedding,
and this spring a fox whelped in the great hall
Careless of the echo of absent lords
There is only the ancient name
now but common parlance for this stunted copse

We still teach our children, in fairy tales and legends
of the wise man of the wood
Bringing wisdom, strength and judgement
protecting the weak, always kind
and when they, innocent, ask
Where are they now, do they live among us still?
Who will admit, we slew them on a whim
for an imagined slight, for base profit

Which among us does not startle
at the shadow of twigs, the gleam in moonlight
Or see, ephemeral in the dusk
the barred ghost we fear still haunts those glades?
And when our children gasp
and speak of strange, furtive figures in the gloom
We hold their hand and say, nay child
It is long and long since badgers last walked here

HEALING

When you have an awful wound, that you don't dare to touch
When you dare not bind or tend it, know that it will hurt too much
Then you gently wash the edges, at the very point of pain
You give a sigh, and brace yourself, and do it all again

It hurts so much to touch it, but deep inside you know
Unless you force yourself do so, it will fester, it will grow
So you grit your teeth, inspect it, it hurts but you must try
to make it clean and healthy, though the pain will make you cry

Then bit by bit it heals, time and care is all it takes
But the scar will always be there, to remind you, when it aches
Mine is a deep and ragged wound, right inside my heart
The legacy of grief and loss, when we were torn apart

I am trying hard to heal it, bind it with such tender care
Wash it often in those gentle, happy memories we shared
Though sure that all our memories and love are here to stay
I can't imagine any future where this pain has gone away

But I'll try, because I know you never meant to bring me pain
and I hope one day I'll heal, and you will make me smile again

HEAR THE DEVIL

On the edges of creation
Myths and nightmares come to play
Waiting for the wild at heart
To tempt them in, then make their day

Smoke it, shoot it, swallow or snort it
Hear the Devil shout in glee
If you want to take a trip
Get the best, get hooked on me

Drive it, fly it, ride it, dive it
Hear the Devil shout with glee
Want to push it to the limit?
Ride the lightning, ride with me

On the edges of creation
Myths and nightmares come to play
Waiting for the wild at heart
To tempt them in, then make their day

Fight it, bite it, beat it, slice it
Hear the Devil shout with glee
Scream or moan, to the bone
Take or give it, fine by me

Sell your body, sell your soul
Hear the Devil shout with glee
We will break all of your chains,
Only you can set you free

On the edges of creation
Myths and nightmares come to play
Waiting for the wild at heart
Come and meet us, make our day

HEARTWOOD

Steeped in years of mirth and pain
of blood-red poppies in fields of grain
Of deep still calm on a moonlit night,
the ecstasy of eagles in flight,
Of hopeless tears, and chances lost,
a million rainbows trapped in frost
Of drunken laughter, a wail of hunger
and lightning tearing heaven asunder

It will not shatter, though it may bend,
and you may break it in the end
But it will hold when all else falls
and always answer when you call
Torn from my breast, laid at your feet
Yours, til it no longer beats
A fist of iron for your velvet glove -
Take this, my heart of oak, my love

HEROIC INDIFFERENCE

A lightening flash, thunder roars
the world cries out in pain
The Beast has risen from the pit
and walks the earth again.
and at his heels the Hounds of Hell
the Werewolf and the Troll
They'll tear your flesh, and break your bones
and the Beast will take your soul
No holy mark, no armour plate
stands up to this attack
Before the fury of his gaze
the Rock of Ages cracks

Rabbi's, imams, priests and prophets
in their squabbling hordes
Unite at last, in disbelief
are dispatched to meet their Lords
The leaders of the world unite
send armies, much too late
Brave soldiers, doomed to disaster
left to meet their fate
Frontiers, treaties, religion, race
no barrier to this foe
A spreading stain across the earth
his growing legions flow

So who will stay his swift advance
Where is the monster's bane?
What Hero, shining bright
will come to cast him down again?
Will the maid contest his progress
with virtue shining bright?
Or will she think those voices
are the drugs she took last night?
And will another Arthur draw
the bright sword from the stone?
Well no, he's killing monsters
on his X-box, safe at home

Humanity runs in screaming swarms
as millions fall and die
Reporters vie for the best shot
to catch a producers eye
With Armageddon coming fast
will we stand up and fight?
No, we'll all go home and watch
the highlights on the news tonight
For TV, dope and mockery
have now prepared the way
Armoured by our indolence
we never even think to pray

The beast rampages outside
we turn on the news and wait
In Heroic Indifference
to watch our approaching fate

HONOUR OF THE REGIMENT

They sent me their assassins
bringing death throughout the night
I place their bodies on the ramparts
where they catch the morning light

They brought fire and destruction
smashing rock and breaking bone
But I was still here, waiting
when the storm of death was done

Cajoling me to yield the way
with bribes and honeyed tones
But I gave my word to hold
and my word is carved and stone

In waves they storm my lines,
but I throw them back again
Now they begin to understand
I am never truly slain

They stamp my banners in the mud
proclaim that I am gone
But I am there to greet them
when the battle-lines are drawn

Behold, I am the Regiment
my honour has no price
I will always be here, waiting
when my country bids me fight

I WISH THAT
THERE WERE DRAGONS

The darkness shot with flaming trails of dragons in the night
Sunlit, rainbow flocks of dragons wheeling, glorious, in flight
Perched on cathedrals, crags and castles, magnificent and proud
and the glint of tiny dragonets, phut phutting through the clouds
Playing hide and seek in thunderstorms, with eagles, sure and swift
Sleeping scattered on the beaches, like washed up jewel-drifts

Without such wondrous creatures, how can this world be whole?
How I wish that there were dragons, to feed magic to my soul

IMAGINATIVE GARDENING

I sow all my little seeds
then stand back to watch them grow
Will they push out roots and branches
or will they swirl and flow?

They grow stronger if you feed them
Imagination is the best
It only takes a drop or two
to add that special zest

You all gave them shape and colour
Made them brighter, bigger, stronger
Perhaps I did inspire them
But now they are mine no longer!

INFANTISUICIDE

And shrieking deep inside you
the child is slowly dying
He's kicking and he's screaming
He's fighting and he's crying

Expectation crushed his bones
and duty bleeds him dry
He is poisoned by ambition -
You can't stop it, though you try

His days were always numbered
from the moment you were born
Your saddest day will be the one
you realise he has gone

INSEPARABLE

Trying to get by day to day
knowing you aren't here to share
Yet still in some strange way
it seems that you are everywhere
Affecting all I say and do
infusing every tiny part,
Saturating all my thoughts
and wrapped right round my heart

IT BEE SPRING

Come on, come on, you sleepy heads
Shake wing and leg, get out of bed
Look at the dust, there's cobwebs too
Patch that crack, yes, that means you
Mum's awake, wants breakfast now
Get some quick, don't care how
Check the cupboards, nearly bare
Need repairs, a new door, there
This nursery, it's such a mess
Clean it up, build more beds
Must go shopping, find more food
Need to feed her hungry brood
Up and away, on balmy air
Natures bounty, everywhere
Flowers on daffy, foxglove, reed
Blossom on every bush, and tree
Back to dance, and twirl, and bow
What we've found, the where, the how
Bulging saddlebags, two by two
Drop by drop, makes golden dew
Buzz busily, bees, make it clear
To all the world, that spring is here

IT'S NOT CRICKET!

"Get off that square!" I hear a cry
it's Mr. Townsend passing by
He's caught me on the cricket square
I really wish I wasn't there
I wouldn't be, but I am late
and haven't time to use the gate
so I sneaked in across the grass
because I love my Latin class
Now I've been caught (that's bad enough)
but worse, I'm on the sacred turf
what can I say, to turn his rage
it isn't safe when you're that age
He's turning green, then pink again
I hope his heart can stand the strain
Speaking of Mr. Townsend's health
I don't feel all that well myself
Oh look! I think that's Mrs. Thickett
She'll get me off this cursed wicket
I'll faint! Oh, yes, salvation's near
I'll faint, they'll take me out of here
I see it now, the tea and rest
(No Mr. Townsend, that's the best!)
He may forget, if given time
but if he can't forgive my crime
and all else fails - I'll volunteer!
to join his cricket team ...... NEXT YEAR

JUST ANOTHER BIRTHDAY

Another birthday over
So another year has gone
Just wish I could remember
Some of what I'd done

If there were superpowers
The one for which I'd pray
Is that I would remember
What I did yesterday

JUST WORDS

You speak of glorious rainbows, and of sunlight on the dew
Stars so bright, the Northern Lights, you swear it all is true
The bright, intricate tapestry, on the wings of a butterfly
The monochrome kaleidoscope as clouds pass in the sky

Autumn leaves come tumbling, as mists enchant the dale
Starlings fill an evening sky, blossoms embroider the vale
Snow that turns our humdrum streets into fairyland overnight
City nightglows overwhelmed by lightning, fierce and bright

Midnight moonlight in a glade, fox caught in depredations
Dolphins reaching for the sky, splashing, crashing exultation
The lustrous scales on gliding trout, a mayflies short, wild dance
The lambent fire in tygers eye, a myriad courting birds entrance

The smile of a child awakening, the glow in a mother's eye
Time, handwritten on ancient faces, lovers, dancers, whirling by
I listen, enraptured, to you, because I have no eyes to see
and so, my garrulous friend, your wonders are just words to me

KITE

Twisting, turning in the air,
bucking, darting everywhere
Easing through the subtle eddy,
waiting, patient, always ready
Updraft, time to soar and swoop,
dying, see my wing tips droop
Diving, building speed and power,
drift on breezes, gentler, slower
Tugging, thrusting to break free,
almost gone, you won't tame me!
Oh no, the tether pulls me lower,
grounded, I hope there's wind tomorrow ...

LAMENT

Autumn Leaves
Falling
Blowing
Drifting
Swirling
Floating
Aimlessly lost

Without you

Chilling
Driving
Pounding
Rain
Scouring
Biting
Numbing
Wind
Rust
Dust
and Desolation

You are gone

LEGACY

Where is it now, that fire that burned in my blood?
Sent me, careless, bare sark, to meet my foe
The battle rage that sweeps me up, and all before
or girds me in the bloody maul of shieldwall

Where is that fierce need to see and know it all?
To follow the dragon, to plough the lonely furrow
Questing, ceaseless, out over the edge of the world
To set my heel on lands unknown, to make them mine

Where is that quick fierce strength, that passion?
Proud to carry the banner of my liege and lord
To dare that lonely death, or the wyms of hel
for my bond, my word, for pride in my given oath

Where is that brave heart, strong to bear me up?
To take my blood and sons, and sons of sons
on across this world, bringing our fire and iron
Writing our claim in lifesblood on the very earth itself

Sons of our true line, surging out to carve the way
Out across the oceans, to spend blood and seed
Leaching the valour, and the spirit, from this isle
Bleeding it's soul, one fierce, wild drop at a time

That potent flood, twined with heroes and kings
Now ebbing, drained by endless spineless prattling
Thieves and lawyers now plunder with impunity
Binding us, helpless, smothered in an insipid web

Still we gather, to drink and speak again of war
But it is a hopeless brew, the fires choked in ash
and though our champions once more step forth
It is surely a sign - they contest but a bag of wind

Is this our heritage now, ancient spirit broken?
While the ghosts of our ancestors helpless rail
Forefathers beat their breasts in impotent rage
and it is only in dreams that I rise
bare sark and bloody-handed once again

LIBERATION

We come to bring liberty
our boys will fight to set you free
and try to only kill one in three
then take your oil to our country
don't need it without roads, you see
no point hiding, or trying to flee
our weapons reach out to infinity
our chemicals kill each bush and tree
and goats and dogs, but accidentally
and poison crops, but charity's free
will dress your children just like me
we'll compensate you, eventually

You'll know as soon as we arrive
when you see children burnt alive
screaming mothers, weeping wives
sons dying of the chemicals imbibed
but at least we will unite your tribes
with hatred, treachery and bribes
and gum for everybody who survives
you can't resist, why do you try?
no need to struggle or to strive
here's a little something to imbibe
we'll save your culture - in our archive
so we can bring you better lives

A LINCOLNSHIRE WELCOME

Potatoes stacked outside the red-brick farm
Carrots, beans, cauliflowers, peas, and corn
No suspicious vendor's stare, no chains or locks
Just please put some money on the box

Magnificent trees strewn, careless, everywhere
Pheasant, hawk and rabbit, ferret, fox and hare
Hedgerows, stitching patchwork quilt of fields
While over hay filled barns, swallow dips and wheels
Slow, deep, lazy rivers, trout lurking in the shallows
Sows with their piglets, asleep, content, in wallows

A slumbering village with a thatched church-gate
Winding lanes, a passing stranger calls you mate
Mallard herds her tiny brood, upon the village pond
Keeper with pint of ale, dog beside him, ancient bond

All these signs, I can relax, at last my journey's done
and Lincolnshire, my Lincolnshire is welcoming me home

LOGICAL ARGUMENT

It started very quietly, no real hint of any bother
I wanted to do one thing, you preferred to do another
You play your opening gambit, so simple, you ask why?
Without a thought I tell you, well at least I start to try

You see through my diversions, trump every card I play
Refuse to be confused, content that logic wins the day
I resort to yet another scheme, try to bribe or flatter
You don't care what I offer, it doesn't seem to matter

When I attempt to push it, demonstrate superior force
You scream and yell and stamp, so I back down, of course
I know you turn it on and off, wish I could find the switch
You've wound me up so tight now, I'm developing a twitch

Those long blonde curly ringlets, flashing eyes of purest blue
With your fluttering eyelashes, mean I can't stay cross at you
When you go on the offensive, I'm just not prepared for that
If we had been wrestling, you'd have pinned me on the mat

Time to surrender, sue for peace, offer an apple or a lolly
Trying to win this dispute was just the height of folly
You stand there with hands on hips, and laugh, triumphantly
I have just lost another argument with a girl who's only three

LOOKING FORWARD

Looking forward now, once more, instead of looking back
Though I never will forget you, no way that I could do that
But just starting to imagine, perhaps I could love again
Fan that little spark of warmth, there, deep within the pain

For without you life is empty, its so lonely, cold and bleak
I look around, an empty space, no answer when I speak
I need to have someone to share, to be with me at night
Someone to bring my smile back, to dissipate my fright

This is going to be difficult, you will understand just why
Although I'll always love you dearly, left alone I can't get by
You are always there, inside me, but I miss your touch the most
Without tactile assurances, I am so confused and lost

I think that I have found someone, can feel my heart expand
at the soft sound of a footfall, feeling warmth beneath my hand
Feeling so much more complete again, without that aching space
As if something that was missing has slipped quietly into place

You are still there, but so is she, it's strange, but it seems true
Where once I had no comforter, somehow I now have two
The comfort of our memories calm me in so many ways
The comfort of her touch gets me through the darkest days

My future is so bright, I clearly see the way ahead
One friend to stand beside me, one always there, inside my head
Together we are so complete, each with a distinctive touch
I feared you'd have to share my love, but there just seems twice as much

LOVE ETERNAL

When the earth becomes a desert,
and all the trees are dead and bare
Though it seems that all has perished,
love will still be blooming there
Through poverty and famine,
when it seems all hope has gone
Our love will warm and nurture us,
until the day hope is reborn

When empires fade and chaos reigns,
when the cities are ablaze
Somewhere safe and hidden,
my love for you remains, always,
Through infection and corruption,
though cruel hatred reigns
Untainted and unblemished,
love will burn, a clear bright flame

When the stars burn down to ashes,
universal cold and dark
My love for you will shine, forever,
one last warm bright spark
If you are lost, or sad and lonely,
wherever you may roam
A bright, clear, shining beacon,
my love will always guide you home

LOVELY WEATHER TODAY

Oh what a lovely day for a walk in the sun
We don't get many, make the most of this one
An azure dome over everyone
Butterflies, Bees, a background hum
Oh what a beautiful day for a walk in the sun

How I love to splash in the pouring rain
Getting wet doesn't hurt, but people still complain
Washing away grime and stains
One drop at a time, pristine again
How I love to go walking out in the pouring rain

Have you ever been out alone in the morning mist?
When a breeze on your cheek becomes a chilly kiss
Familiar that blurring into this
Every step a whole world missed
Have you ever been out alone to be lost in the mist?

What a treat to go roaming out in fresh deep snow
A coat of pristine white over all that I know
The whole world frozen in mid-flow
The light has an ethereal glow
The joys of playing out in the falling snow

Have you ever breathed in deep of a moonlit night?
With all the heavens bejewelled with starfields bright
When the shadows are deep
and the world is asleep
All the subtle scents of a clear and moonlit night

See the turbulence of clouds of a sky in pain
Wince as thunder and lightning batter the brain
Winds scour the plain
and great trees strain
Under turbulent clouds in a thunderous sky of pain

But best of them all, is a day long gone
With you in my arms, sun-kissed, wind-blown
When time is undone
When I'm not alone
Oh, what would I give, for one day long gone?

MARION THE MOLEHUNTER

Marion the mole hunter crouched in the grass
Waiting for moles to come wandering past
If only one came within range of her club
That long pointy nose would be only a stub

Everywhere you could see a mole hole
Because Maurice the Mole was on a roll
He had his sights set on Marion's lawn
So much to get done before the dawn

Then Maurice the Mole had a terrible scare
Without any warning, Marion was there!
Her hair full of brambles, covered in mud
Mo started digging as fast as he could

Down came the club, but Maurice had gone
When it comes to digging he is number one
Marion stomped off, to sleep until day
At least, she thought, I have scared him away

But alas, it was clear in the cold light of dawn
Maurice had molehilled Marion's lawn
They went first, they stood no chance
Stamped in Marion's frenzied war-dance

She raided the internet, eBay and such
Buying equipment, spent way too much
When it arrived, Marion grimly predicted
Maurice the Mole would be interdicted

There were fiendish traps to put in holes
Sprays that were instant death to moles
There were springs to fling them out of tunnels
Quick-setting jelly to squirt through funnels
Bio-engineered bloodsucking roots
A hand-made set of mole-charming flutes
Muskets that fired mole-hunter darts
Poisons baked into crispy worm tarts
Napalm pellets with 10 second fuses
and several convicted mole abusers
Powders to irritate mole epiderms
Gunpowder eating kamikaze worms
Clockwork hammers to squash Maurice flat
and Marion's favourite, a big spiky bat.

They filled the shed, the kitchen too
The lounge, the bedroom, even the loo
Once she worked out what each one was for
She put on her wellies and went off to war

First, she knew it made lots of sense
When fighting a war, to have a defence
She dug a trench all around the grass
Filled with gravel so moles couldn't pass

But Maurice is more than an average mole
He earned his stripes by mining coal
So gravel beds didn't stop him at all
With bark he lined the roof and wall

He shouldn't have been so sure of himself
Marion had left him something else
He got shakes and shivers, a queasy belly
The gravel was soaked in noxious jelly!

Marion knew her reprieve wouldn't last
Maurice the mole would recover too fast
She started installing the traps and such
Her neighbours thought it was much too much

She laid trails of worms, an occasional wriggly
Although tying them fast was terribly fiddly
Then out across her smooth green lawn
Marion's battle-line was drawn

She dug out the pits, used a biscuit tin
So no tunnelling out once Maurice was in
Covered them over with grass and branches
Sawn part through to increase her chances

She put bundles of flypapers in the tree
With cotton tripwires, to pull them free
Puddles of syrup to muddle mole-feet
Surrounding a tempting minced-worm treat

Heat-seeking catapults near the roses
Cameras to catch embarrassing poses
Axes in devilishly devious trajectories
Nail scissors poised for mole vasectomies

The whole lot was crossed by a sensor net
Top of the range, the best she could get
Marion lurked in the nettle patch
Now Maurice the Mole would meet his match

Maurice was ready, revenge on his mind
He intended to do something truly unkind
He'd show her that he'd never be gone
Write Maurice in molehills across the lawn

The postie left lots of elastic bands
Which swiftly became, in Maurice's hands
A trampoline, to project the mole
Out into the garden, no need for a hole

He checked his equipment one last time
Braced himself to cross the line
The time had come, so expecting the worst
He activated his Mole Hunter curse

He had his maps, and a folding stool
A first World War entrenching tool
A sword he found on a Time Team dig
Skeleton keys and his lock-picking twig

A medal his grandad won in the trenches
Welsh miners penknife, a couple of wrenches
A professional cockroach for sniffing gases
His magnifying infra-red glasses

With various drills, and his lucky pick
An antique brass-bound dousing stick
A cat-seeking crossbow, his own invention
because overkill was Mo's intention

One big bounce, he soared through the skies
Came zooming in, a total surprise
Dressed to kill, like a cinema hero
Maurice the Mole arrived at ground zero!

But temptation came from every direction
Mole treats laid out for his inspection
He was very suspicious, but hungry too
Poor Maurice just had to try a few

Disaster! He crashed into a pit
His pogo boots bounced him out of it
Assassin wasps zoomed into the fray
He released a cricket to lure them away

Poison gas - he should have been dead
But he had a fish bowl over his head
The radar had him locked in its sights
Until he engaged his super-stealth tights

Catapults twanged, and rocks filled the air
He dodged and he danced with incredible flair
One knocked his shield clean out of his hand
The next was lower, he was nearly unmanned

But Maurice knew he was facing defeat
No choice - he began a fighting retreat
Marion was sure he'd elude and evade her
She pulled the Armageddon lever !!

Up came the springs, traps were sprung
Maurice the Mole had no chance to run
Glued and netted, shot and suspended
Maurice's final mole-run was ended

Marion leapt out, triumphant at last
Maurice would soon be a mole of the past
She intended to make him Maurice squash
But as she swung that big spiky cosh ...

Maurice looked up, a tear in his eye
A mole in his prime, too young to die
She looked in his eyes, a fatal pause ....
She couldn't kill Maurice now, of course

She ranted, stamped, threw her club away
Tried to decide what to do with her prey
She looked round her garden and realised
The mole couldn't ruin it more if he tried

She had dug up nearly all of the grass
The flower beds were a thing of the past
The veggie patch was a minefield now
She'd do less damage using plough

So she pulled poor Maurice out of the mess
Untied him and bandaged his arm and his chest
Scrubbed him until all the glue was gone
and then, of course, put the kettle on

She gave our Maurice a beetle bun
(sure that it wasn't a poisoned one)
Sipped her tea, and thought it through
There was only one thing she could do

Marion has hung up her mole-hunter spade
Maurice repaired the mess that she'd made
They both made a deal that fateful dawn
He would never molehill Marion's lawn

Now Maurice the mole is a happy boy
Marion's veggie patch his to enjoy
Marion still clubs the occasional slug
A treat for Mo, for the acres he's dug

But Marion lives in her garden shed
The house is home to her mole traps instead
How could she sell them to some passing stranger
and put some innocent mole in danger?

Though the mole abusers were taken away
The poisonous stuff is here to stay
The explosives might come in handy, its true
and ants have been eating the syrup and glue

But Marion isn't the type to whine
She makes a few quid, in her spare time
The traps and spikes will not find their target
Become modern art to sell at the market

So next time you gather your weapons of war
Try talking, to get what you're looking for
While the deal you make may not be truly fair
It helps if one party is tied to a chair

MEMORIES

On sad and lonely days, when you feel lost in endless night
A happy memory can be your only source of light
So cherish happy memories, although they cause you pain
and in your the darkest hour, they will light your way again

Sometimes, through the sadness, they can even make you smile
So search for them, enjoy them, let them warm you for a while
Cherish each precious moment, make them your treasure trove
Until you're walking in their light, with everyone you've loved

MESSENGER

The hero falls, but the battle's won
Threat to homes and families gone
But of these deeds no-one has heard
Someone must swiftly spread the word

Her moment now has come, at last
Too small to stand in the cannon's blast
Yet eager to play some special part
Prove her courage and steadfast heart

She spread her wings and flew away
From the debris of that desperate fray
Put her prow to the shores of home
Plotted her track o'er the endless foam

Through gales that tore her ropes and stays
Driven by storms, swamped by the waves
Stranded, with a faintest hint of breeze
Steadfastly on, across endless seas

Though battered and torn, a welcome sight
Through the driving rain, her harbour lights
But the wind came up, a cruel jest
Kept her from anchorage, home, and rest

When she finally made it to her berth
Tied tight at last to her native earth
The people wept, and the people cheered
News they hoped for, news they'd feared

Late that night by the harbour wall
She lay, alone, forgotten by all
Proud of her passage, her duty done
A messenger who's race was run

Remembered those she would see no more
Shattered and broken on distant shores
Shattered and broken by iron and fire
Their billowing sails their funeral pyre

Those hearts of oak, those famous names
Those great proud ships will not fight again
Scattered on far-flung ocean's floor
To keep the foe from Britannia's door

When next the fleet hoves into view
Some battered friends, tried and true
So many missing, a price was paid
The coin of freedom, a cruel trade

No-one staggering to rum-soaked bed
Saw salt-stained tracks on her figurehead
There in the harbour, the Pickle, alone
Wept for all the ships that were gone

Pickle was the ship that brought the news of the victory at Trafalgar,
and the death of Nelson, back to England.

MIDNIGHT PASSIONS

Long, lean, lovely limbs
Tangled in my mind, and in my sheets
Entwining nerves and senses
My reason fleeing in defeat

Now heating blood and brain,
Burning through both memory and will
Darker need rises, urges my excess
Now urgent, seeking for a deeper thrill

and hot wet velvet on my lips
Soft warm skin slides over and around
Surrendering and conquering my all
Harsh ragged breath, the only sound

On eagles wings, up, to meet the lightning strike
Sharp sweet pain, the rainbow's gentle kiss
Then, damp on skin and lips
Passion fails, darkness brings oblivion's bliss

Awakening to chill damp grubby sheets
Dull grey morning light
To know it all was naught
Just another long, cold, sad and lonely night

MIND GAMES

Caught up in a web of lies
First he struggles, then he dies
A victim of the jaws of steel
Never seen her? Pray you never will

Spawned on floods of bitter tears
Nurtured on your secret fears
Growing stronger, saps your will
Soon you're ready for the kill

Broken bodies, broken minds
Mark the victims of her kind
Scourge of woman, bane of man
Conscience never stays her hand

Keep your guard up, just one slip
and she will have you in her grip
Once she has you, time to play
Struggle harder - Make Her Day!

Her lair is not in graveyard's gloom
In sepulchre or broken tomb
Among you, now, there lives the beast
This hunter needs a living feast

In the corners of your mind
Live the children of her kind
Midst the memories you have lost
Spent emotions, gone to rust
Sifting dust of yesteryear
Tainting all that you hold dear

Walk in the sun, show no fear
The slightest doubt, and she'll be here
Spinning webs of hesitation
Once she has you - No Salvation!

MOONSTRUCK

Now the sun god he's a'dying
Falling down, down out of sight
And the goddess is set free
to fly up, up above the night

And my soul once more is yearning
to fly to her cold embrace
And scream my helpless passions
before her cold and cruel face

Deep in darkness I can hear her
and her siren voice cuts deep
So deep into my solitude
Overwhelming will and sleep

Queen of all who shun the light
Who only dream of dark, and night
Fleeing now from greater might
Dawn, the sun shines oh, too bright!

Pallid Mistress of desires
Temptress stoking unholy fires
The Angel who brought exhultation
Gone! My world is desolation

MULTITUDES SPRING FORTH

Dib dib dib, long straight lines, a myriad tiny bright green stitches
Farmers sewing patches on Mother Nature's ragged britches
Splinters, grit, a lot of spit, Bees and Wasps permit no shirkers
Dormitories will be needed, for mother's teeming, buzzing workers

Sneezing, snorting, coughing, enduring endless, sleepless night
While Pollens swirl in exultation, join the great fertility rite
A cloud of scarlet micro dots burst from cracks and under ledges
Ladybirds are hunting aphids over gardens, fields and hedges

Croaking, hopping, clambering, squirming, filling everything with spots
Froggies spawning jellied eggs in ponds, puddles and rain-filled pots
Buzzing, biting, stabbing, sucking, a billion hungry mothers fly
All driven on by procreation, trying to suck the whole world dry

Flocking, fluttering, soaring high, musical combat, or love-matching
Digging, mending, building, lining, cribs prepared for early hatching
Fields and gardens are alive, with wiggly chomping munching things
Impatient caterpillars, growing, dream of flight on rainbow wings

A galaxy of bright new faces lift to greet the coming dawn
Daisies, dandelions and buttercups, bejewel meadows and your lawn
An eager host of spirits rise, a myriad hearts are beating fast
As we rise from our beds to find that Spring is bursting forth, at last!

THE NAMING OF DEITIES

When mankind looked for deities, to worship from afar
First they tried the sun, the wind, prayed to a shooting star
But as their knowledge grew, they needed something more
Some mystery to explain exactly what this life is for

The first ones that they tried, were like a very strict old dad
Promising fire and brimstone, for every bit of fun they had
It did not take too long before they got fed up with that
They tried serene, indifferent, they tried cheerful and fat

Then somebody suggested, got lots of others to concur
We'll decide what type of deity, that we would all prefer
We want someone to love us, was the first thing on the list
No matter what awful things we've done, on that we must insist
and if we are cruel or thoughtless, if we sin or if we stray
We want a warm and loving welcome, though we don't care anyway
We'll show no gratitude, but we want comfort in our sorrow
No blame, and no rejection, when we sin again tomorrow
Acceptance of all offerings, sporadic, stale, or cheap
Must be always there when needed, must watch over us in sleep

So they refined all of the details, they argued and debated
Found one example of the deity they wished to see created
They could not use its actual name, that would have seemed quite odd
and so they spelt it backwards, chose the perfect name of - GOD

NIGHTMARE

mist, lazy, slow, stealthy, drowning sight and sound
insubstantial, ethereal carpet smothering the ground
flickering, hidden hints of unseen watchers, all around
tendrils lend life to limb and leaf, ancient fear unbound

glistening droplets swell each stem and leaf with bloat
seem to ooze from moss and bark, the world afloat
each breath fighting for air, damp fingers in the throat
stifles speech, dulls senses - something insidious gloats

sensation fading slowly from numbed fingers and toes
chill creeping, slides unheeded through sodden clothes
clumsy, stumbling, leaden limbs, heart stutters, slows
sense and will now faltering, helpless desperation grows

burst of light and sound, voices, drives the chill from bones!
held fast in strong, warm, arms, childhood terrors gone
nightmares shattered, scattered, into oblivion blown
lingering terrors, fading, lurk - 'til I am once more alone

ONE TRUE THING

Atoms reborn into grass
Fire and passion stilled at last
Clouds, of happy what might be's
Scattered showers of grief and tears
Fading memories, not quite true,
One day, my friend, this will be you

PACK

Before I step into the dark
I'll call to the dogs long gone
Of loyalty, and love, and faith
and the good times we have known

So when I take my first small step
in the land beyond my death
I'll hear them howling welcome
'ere I can draw a breath

For love cuts deep, and blood means kin
and both form a potent pact
But neither is as deep and strong
as the ties that bind the pack

PASSING STRANGERS

Eye catching eye, hesitant, searching,
as recognition flickers, uncertain
Almost familiar, so many times glimpsed,
a ghost behind memory's curtain
Tangled mane of hair, so pale,
colours leached away in endless flow of time
Stories of life, laughter and tears,
each tale etched deep, line by careworn line
Pallid, unshaven cheek, white speckled,
age painted onto chin and scrawny throat,
Shoulders, hunched in anticipation of the past,
sheltering in threadbare coat
That glum, turned-down mouth, softening,
twitching, mirth now tints the fears,
Soft lips on tanned skin murmur through the muffling,
stifling weight of years
Rain spattering, smearing into oblivion
that sorrowful gaze, dull with old pain
Recoiling, I flee reflection,
haunted by the certainty that we will meet again

PEEWIT

Swooping, soaring, diving, in scintillating, whirling mirth
Bright, colourless jesters, mocking gravity of mind and earth
A twist, a turn and now, Black Baron plummets from on high
Challenges all to battle, claims dominance of this spring sky
Screaming his two-tone defiance of daring, nimble foes
Dauntless, steadfast, defending, the precious stony patch he chose
Forsaking sleep, scorning fatigue, raging storm, and food
Preserving this barren plot, perfect home for incipient brood

Hiatus. She comes! Serene, indifferent, Queen of all desires
A pause, then tumbling, whirling clouds of suitors paint the skies
Monochrome kaleidoscopic whirl, the Baron is through, and past
Trails the scarlet banner of his dominance, unchallenged at last
Triumphant, he scatters all, then, gentle, diffident, changing pace
Tempting, luring, pleading, extolling virtues of this barren place
He leads, the first tentative steps, enticing her to join the dance
She feigns indifference, glides over his palace, deigns to glance
He leads her to his fortress, proud of each stick and stubborn stone
Bows, scrapes, pleading for her to consent, to make this her home
Encouragement! or not? He circles closer, radiates magnificence
She decides, consents, submits. Tempo rises, faster, intense
They flaunt their acrobatic amour, an aerial duet, rising ever higher
Each now claims the other, in a ballet of passion and desire

Now content, she takes her throne, as he patrols, guards her well
Beneath her, their sparks of immortality, safe in armoured shell

PEREGRINE

To soar above the thunderclouds has always been your legacy
To stoop at speeds unmatched as you close upon your prey
To twist and jink round salt-stained sea stacks drenched in foam
To pit your strength and awesome skill against the raging storm

Behold this spectacle, this glorious, exuberant freedom
is not in mountain wilderness, safe from our depredation
Blessed we are, you have brought your wild exultation
into this arid concrete wasteland, our heart of desolation

All that is yet a promise, trapped inside this fragile shell
and I wish that I could send to the deepest pits of hell
Those who would hoard your casket where none but they can see
or raise you, caged, to serve their will, never to fly free

POPPY PARADE

Once more we gather, the great parade,
for faithful comrades, friend, and foe
The bands wait silent to do their part,
drum and bugle, measured and slow
This day is for the heroes bold,
and the broken cowering in the mud
Those noble born, or raised in slums,
brothers forever now joined in blood

We bow our heads and, silent,
weep our crimson petals on hill and dale
and once more paint the fields with red,
o'er Verdun, Ypres, and Paschendale

REACTIONS

Who can foresee how they will face it,
their reactions on the day
When dreams come down in ruins,
their beloved is torn away
Some will grieve alone for ever,
some will one day love again
Some will hold their memories close,
some will try to share the pain

No matter your reactions,
for us all one thing holds true
The fact that we react at all,
is why our loved ones loved us too

DARK KNIGHT (REDEMPTION)

I never was a shining hero, on a charger pure and white
but that was how you saw me, when I held you in the night
When I banished all your nightmares, kept your fears at bay
Stood between you and the darkness, until the dawn of day

In my memory are many deeds that you must never know
My selfish, craven silence gave your love a chance to grow
In the warm of your devotion, though my scars will never heal
A spark of love began to grow, this I never thought to feel

I'm not looking for forgiveness, or for the world to understand,
Accept me as you see me, I just want to be your man
I don't deserve a second chance, never tried to take the first
But for you I'll give my very best, and you'll never see my worst

You tamed my inner demons, bound them with your chains of love
Tenderly wrapped my iron fists in a gentle velvet glove
Brought your light into my darkness, soothed my troubled soul
and in one moment of redemption, made my shattered spirit whole

Now you have gone into the dark, left me in endless night
But your love, there in the rising tide, is a beacon shining bright
A storm of rage is pushing hard, but for you I hold my ground
and the memory of you, smiling, still keeps my demons bound

RIDING WITH THE ANGELS

Shining bright behind your eyes, where only you can see
The angels wait to ride the night, and set your spirit free

The weather really brings you down, nothing seems quite right,
You find no-one agrees with you, then you really get uptight
Behind that gloomy edifice, turn on your inner light
No need to take it anymore, its time to turn and fight
Put on your lace and lycra, and paint your colours bright
Go riding with the angels, down the freeways of the night

The boring job, the stingy boss, the computer that broke down
Workmates with wandering hands, that annoying office clown
You bow your head and soldier on, with your feet firm on the ground
But though you play their games, don't let it always hold you down
Put on your fur and feathers, spray your colours all around
Then ride with the angels of the night, and really paint the town

Shining bright behind your eyes, where only you can see
The angels wait to ride the night, and set your spirit free

They bind you with the chains of love, think you're bought and sold
Every way you twist and turn, they seem to stop you cold
The job, the family, social life, they put you in a mould
No need to fear the loneliness, you can always break that hold
Just put on chains and leathers, and paint your colours bold
They can never stop you riding free, down the highways of your soul

They steer decision with 'advice', believe they're being kind
Your clothes and hair, your look and style, controlled all of the time
But your spirit can't be fettered, and your soul they cannot bind
for although they chain your body, you can always cross that line
Just put on your your studs and denim, and boldly paint your sign
Take a road trip with the angels, through the byeways of your mind

Shining bright behind your eyes, where only you can see
The angels wait to ride the night, and set your spirit free

RITE OF WAY

There's only one trouble with driving a car
You meet other cars if you drive very far
No matter how carefully you drive your truck
Some idiot will always be pushing their luck

They drive too fast and frighten the kids
Navigate corners with screeches and skids
Play music that rouses your granny at nights
Follow too closely while flashing their lights

They overtake lorries around blind bends
Block narrow roads for miles without end
Use three parking spaces and never pay
Act as if we are the ones in the way

Beep hooters just to signal their friend
Give no signal to show us what they intend
or they indicate right for mile after mile
Sit at junctions for an awful long while

Somehow the camera misses their crime
They zoom through red lights, time after time
But you know the thing that is worst by far?
They are much too young for such a nice car !!!!

RUN FOR YOUR LIVES

Run for your lives, that engine's coming fast
All those sparks and cinders will set fire to the grass
Soon your homes and gardens will be drifting clouds of ash
Run for your lives, the railway's coming past !!

Run for your lives, before it rolls right over you
The horses were too slow, so they made them into glue
They're building motorways, so the cars can race straight through
So run for your lives, before you're under tarmac too !!

Run for your lives, or get on your knees and pray
They're tearing down the hedgerows, taking all the trees away
With tractors they are smashing every burrow, nest and dray
Run for your lives, we'll all die here if we stay !!

Run for your your lives, even though you're cold and wet
Their boats have engines too, this must be the worst day yet
Deafening whales and dolphins, and dragging great big nets
Run for your lives, as far away as you can get !!

Run for your lives, though I don't know where to hide
Those smelly, noisy engines are now racing through the skies
Frightening the birdies, squashing bees and butterflies
No point running now, this time I'm sure we're going to die !!

No more running now, we are safe although it's true
I'd rather be still running, than locked up, here in this zoo
They're building over all the green, and polluting all the blue
All stone and smoke and noise, no place to run for me and you.

THE SAGA OF SID THE SARDINE

Sid the Sardine was a naughty young lad
Disobedient and rude, but not really bad
One day on the seabed a bottle he found
Tugged off the top, swam in, and around

It had such a strange effect on our Sid
He kept on extolling the good that it did
He wanted more, became almost frantic,
Then a shark, attracted by Sid's crazy antics
said I'll tell you where there's a lot of that stuff
you've got a bad habit, but there'll be enough!

He took our Sid miles, right up to the shore
Sid found a taste, he wanted much more
So he followed the scent, our intrepid hero
Found lots more sardines, laid out in a row
They said, this place, it is truly fantastic
Theres plenty for all, so lie down with us, quick

He lay with the rest, with his mouth open wide
The tin lid came down, trapped our poor Sid inside
I'm sure you've all guessed, the moral of this sonnet
Don't drink from a bottle that says 'ketchup' on it

SANTA'S POSTMEN

We all see fancy carvings on the castle, church and keep
Well, once a year, on Christmas Eve, when we are all asleep
They all rouse up at Rudolph's call, burst into glorious flight
Glittering, shining messengers, lighting up the Christmas night

You all thought t'was elves and fairies, but truth is stranger yet
Thank Santa's gargoyle postmen, for all the presents that you get
Zipping down your chimneys, or in through your letter box
Leaving glowing trails of magic as they race against the clock

When all is done they gather round, to sing and dance and boast
and a special treat of warm fresh milk, and buttered dragon toast
Then they fly back, colours fading, as they feel the magic leave
To dream of soaring through the night, and to wait for Christmas Eve

SAVE A SPACE

In a clearing in the woodland, stands a little wooden shack
with a babbling brook beside it, and a meadow at the back.
I can tell that someone who loves animals lives here
by the cat hair in the cobwebs, and on bushes, clumps of fur
A jet black one-eyed cat perched in that tree, just out of reach
and a big wet hairy wolf, running up from a golden beach
There's a big fat ginger moggy, curled up on a rocking chair
a semi-siamese is lurking, in the shadows over there
A breathing hump of golden fur, kittens, playing and sleeping
Eye opens, checks all kitties are still safely in his keeping

That rocking chair out on the porch, no-one around, and yet
Crocheted squares scattered on it, for a cat blanket, I'd bet
Balls of wool everywhere, twitch among them, nearly blended
Green eyes blaze, black mohair animates, illusion ended
Two slim gleaming, racing, forms flow smoothly over the sward
Ears pricked, checking, scenting, to see if ought is untoward
Burst into exuberant, gleeful, mass of rippling muscle wriggling
Great black whiplash thrashing, brown stump frantic, waggling
White flash, claws run gently up my legs and on my shoulder
When this purring puss wants fuss, there is no-one bolder
Insistent, demanding call, I turn and smile, a persistent habit
There in the grass, Huxley the hunter is enjoying a tasty rabbit
Great black beast sits waiting, with leg and nose of gleaming white
waits impatient, but Hux raised him, so they never fight
From every side they come, an avalanche of love and memories
Meeper, Jemma, Mopsy, Nermal, PumPum, I know all of these
Walking out into the sun, four-legged friends on every side
Movement, there, within the shack, the door is open wide

My love awaits, kitten-swathed, with Mel laid close by
Smiles a welcome, bids me sit, saved a space there at her side

THE SCALE OF A DRAGON

I went to fill the bird feeder, and much to my surprise
There was a dragon watching me, with crimson glittering eyes
At first I thought, April Fool, a toy, somebody's joke
Then he swam across the birdbath, chirped, and I saw smoke
When he rooted in the seed tray, I was really at a loss
He chose his grain, produced a flame, presto! Dragon toast

They still tease me about dragons, but I no longer care
'cos now I know, I see the signs of dragons everywhere
They play on the edge of rainbows, in the sparkle of the dew
If you believe in dragons, you can find them close to you

Look for them at any time, but springtime seems the best
When I think the little dragonets grow up and leave the nest
They are just a little clumsy, leave burnt seed upon the mat,
Tiny scorches in the grass, and singe the whiskers on your cat

THE SEANCE

It all began last Halloween
a drunken, foolish boast
We all went to the Seance
to catch ourselves a ghost

We all sat round the table
while the medium cast her spell
We all held hands as I asked
for a Fiend straight out of Hell

All at once the whole Earth moved
my heart began to race
A voice whispered "I love you"
and then I saw your face

Were you sent to steal my soul
to snare me with your charms?
I'd send my soul to Hell right now
to hold you in my arms

For in that moment I was lost
my whole world fell apart
You blew my mind, you smiled, and then
you stole away my heart

I've dealt the Cards, I've cast the Runes
I've gazed in a Crystal Ball
Tried every spell in every book
but I found no Sign at all

I'll make a pact with Gabriel
and a deal with Satan too
So I can search through Heaven
and Hell, 'til I find you

SIMPLE SOLUTIONS

Nuclear nations hesitate, waiting to see who will move first
Green Peace prevaricates, won't say which fate is worst
The UN sends more diplomats to report what they discover
The Pope, deep in the Vatican, issues one bull after another
Al Queda blame a western plot, Imams say it's literate women
Minor religions all rejoice, claim this time it's their god coming

Science advisors can't agree on just what science to employ
Hedonists don't have a plan, except to go out and enjoy
Philosophers prevaricate about exactly what it means
Naturists don't care much, as long as it is labelled green
The local council meets to see what bye-laws cover this
Some starlet brought photographers, hoping for a publicity kiss

Newspapers craft headlines, telling us what's wrong
Reporters fill the pages with sport and television songs
Planners draw up schedules, to cover any situation
Bankers soothe our fears, scurry off to tax-free nations
Negotiators talk, try to connect, with calmness, and with tact
Politicians offer manifestos, carefully avoiding fact

Public works build loos and tents, for we surely need ablutions
in all of this THE ONLY ONES TO COME UP WITH A SOLUTION

SINNER?

You say I am a sinner
but that's your God's rules, not mine
and I don't expect I'll see him
when it comes to Judgement Time

SISTERS OF MERCY

The chill of evening spreads a cloak
across the bloody battle-plain
Hides all signs of slaughter,
but the sounds of agony and prayin'
Sisters of Mercy come at last,
spread silence like a stain
With a kiss to soothe the terror,
and a knife to end the pain

THE SKIES OF LINCOLNSHIRE

Beneath the skies of Lincolnshire let me live out my days
Where horizons fade in distance, into inconsequential haze

Scattered breezes playing, chasing zephyrs to and fro
Billowing, towering, nimbus, building Camelots of snow
Gods of storm and thunder come to play on days like these
When thunderbolts, bright aliens, stalk careless through the trees

Summer with the blazing sun, triumphant, shining through
Angels painting heaven's dome a flawless eggshell blue
Swirling mists, their ghost graffiti chart the atmospheric flow
The darkening weight of evening crushes sunset's final glow

My personal planetarium, a billion diamonds shining bright
Where shooting stars exclaim! at the sheer immensity of night
The crimson blades of dawn that slash the skirts of night away
Skeins of geese stitch tapestries across the endless grey
Washed-out streaks of winters morn, hint of snow clouds yet to come

The ever-changing immensity of the skies that bring me home

SLITHERY SNAKE'S SNACK

Mummy Duck out on the lake
Five little ducklings in her wake
Slithery Snake looking for a snack
Hears them all, calling Quack
Quack! Quack! Quack! Quack! Quack!

Slithery Snake swims at the back!
Slithery Snake is getting his snack
Slithery's open mouth goes snap!
Quack! Quack! Quack! Quack!

Slithery Snake still wants a snack
One little bump in the middle of his back
Slithery's open mouth goes snap!
Quack! Quack! Quack!

Slithery Snake still wants a snack
Two little bumps in the middle of his back
Slithery's open mouth goes snap!
Quack! Quack!

Slithery Snake still wants a snack
Three little bumps in the middle of his back
Slithery's open mouth goes snap!
Quack!

Slithery Snake still wants a snack
Four little bumps in the middle of his back
Slithery's mouth gives a snap!
Mummy Duck turns round, no Quack?

Mummy Duck starts to flap
Sees the lumps in Slithery's back
Opens her beak and gives a QUACK!!!
Chases Slithery onto the track

Parkie Jim comes down the track
Sees five bumps in Slithery's back
Scoops up Slithery in a sack
Squeezes Slithery's tummy - Quack?
Quack!

One little duckling gives a Quack
Four lumps now in Slithery's back
Another tummy squeeze and - Quack?
Quack! Quack!

Two little ducklings give a Quack
Three lumps now in Slithery's back
Another tummy squeeze and - Quack?
Quack! Quack! Quack!

Three little ducklings give a Quack
Two lumps now in Slithery's back
Another tummy squeeze and - Quack?
Quack! Quack! Quack! Quack!

Four little ducklings give a Quack
One lump left in Slithery's back
Another tummy squeeze and - Quack?
Quack! Quack! Quack! Quack! Quack!

Mummy Duck out on the lake
Five little ducklings in her wake
Swimming close behind her back
Quack! Quack! Quack! Quack! Quack!

Slithery Snake going down the track
Slithery Snake still needs a snack
But now he's got out of the sack
Slithery Snake will never come back!

SONG OF A LIFE

His blood sings loud within him
Rhythm of spring, beating life's drum
He gambols in carefree innocence
No thought of future, of what may come

He screams the passion of eagles
Flaunts his power with each wingbeat
Dancing through the heart of the storm
The tumbling ballet of love's first heat

His heart sings the song of the wild, wild wolf
Hunting through the cold, dark night
Guarding his den and feeding his mate
Playing with pups in the pale moonlight

He bellows a story of glories now past
Of bulls defeated, of calves he has sired
But his broken tusks weigh heavily now
He wanders alone, and his heart is tired

In the soft caress of the oceans deep
He sings his last, sad song to the past
Scarred by battles with squid and man
He turns his head to the beach at last

His soul sings the song of winter's cold
Of the ache of scars and the creeping years
He sings of a life lived full and well
Of laughter, of love, and the memory of tears

The breeze still whispers of memories
Storms shout of deeds and passion gone
In the echo of silence on calm still nights
In the laugh of a child, we hear his song

SORROW

There's one more cloud in the sky today
and one less star at night
The rain is colder, the wind blows keener
the sun doesn't shine as bright.

STARMAN

Millennia have passed since my oh-so distant kin
Last felt the heat of sol beat down upon their skin
But still a yellow sun brings me a golden tan
DNA remembering, I am born the seed of man

Billions of miles away, straight up into the sky
Generations yet to come will listen to this cry
Ethereal postcard, obedient to ancient will
Their prodigal children remembering them still

Star-struck, footloose vagabonds, moon-kissed
Fled into the trackless dark, barely missed
Strove for the stars, abandoned gravity and fear
To be free again, the first across this last frontier

Burning fiery trails across the endless dark
Humanities seed and spirit in each fragile ark
Adapting, blending, joining that Darwinian dance
Warped by alien suns, homo sapiens' last chance

Hurling across the universe in my tiny metal berth
Tenuous, fragile links persist, to that primeval hearth
Rhythmic, hypnotic lullaby, echoes of the deep
The tides of mother earth still rock me gently into sleep

THE GUNS
(DANCE WITH THE DEVIL)

Call for our assistance and we'll give the buggers hell
But ask for close support, then you'd better dig in well
Though you give the right co-ordinates, expect a little slap
We give 'em their directions, but a shell can't read a map
Then load and fire, load and fire, fast as a gun can take
an' it's open sights, and canister, and pray the bastards break

You can dream of dusky maidens, sweat and passion in the dark
But don't kiss the gunner's daughter, you will always wear her mark
It's the line troops get the medals, but if they lose they claim
that Artillery was late or missed, an' the gunner gets the blame
But when the Devil's closing in, the guns won't let you down
Then it's plunging fire, and air bursts, and God will know his own

If you are dancing with the Devil, don't let the bastard lead
'cos if you let him set the step, you know you gotta bleed
The guns can always keep the beat, asleep or when they're pissed
if the Devil wants to dance our tune, he'll know that he's been kissed
So keep step with the gunner, and always mark your exit well
Dancin' the gunner's 'excuse me' means breakfast time in hell

THE OTHERS

His name and rank will not be found,
carved on gleaming blocks of stone
On tablets raised on hallowed ground,
or forgotten corners, overgrown
His name is not in mouldering tomes,
recording all our fallen brothers
Not one of those who ne'er came home,
he is just - - - one of the others

The promise of his bright young life,
given at his country's call
Although he came back from the strife,
body and mind, it cost him all
When peace was signed they sent him home,
gave him a medal, and turned away
Their war is over, but all alone,
he stills re-lives it, every day

For Donald Shillito and all those others who gave their tomorrows,
then had to live through them

THIS FLAG IS STONED

('inspired' by Bruce Springstein)

Wherever this flag is flown
it is spat on, burnt and stoned
this flag should not have gone
it should have stayed at home
taken care of just our own
our flag's reputation is blown
now we should care for our own

Election time they always plead
they're the one we should heed
stories to make your heart bleed
within each lie a little seed
a truth, to make us all believe
they are the one who will succeed
the one who truly cares for our own
they don't even care for their own

The politicians heart is stone
they tax us, bleed us to the bone
then, when all our money's gone
the bankers come, take your home
leave you broke, and all alone
where each precious child was born
where once this flag was flown
where I once took care of my own
who will take care of our own?

Wherever this flag is flown
it is spat on, burnt and stoned
this flag should not have gone
it should have stayed at home
taken care of just our own
our flag's reputation is blown
now we should care for our own

The rich, they know what to do
pay no taxes, unlike me and you
they donate to a politician who
pays a little to the party too
soon it don't matter who is who
cos money tells them what to do
they just push their own law through
and TV says what it's told to
our kids will never know what's true
in the land where this flag flew
where once the wind of freedom blew

preaching charity to everyone
they take it all and give us none
disbelief and the heathen growin'
pretty soon all our faith is blown
they don't even care for their own
so any chance for us is gone
church is open but is God home?
or does He just care for His own

Wherever this flag is flown
it is spat on, burnt and stoned
this flag should not have gone
it should have stayed at home
taken care of just our own
our flag's reputation is blown
now we should care for our own

They always know what's best for you
TV tells you - so it must be true
sells you crap you'll never need
tells you it will make you free
we give coupons to trailer trash
so they will work cheap for cash
fill their sons with crack and hash
teach them hate, but not to wash

Teach their daughters to get rich
by posing nekkid for some pics
the pimp makes them his bitch
the rich buy them with the glitz

no charge for basic education
but we teach nothing of fornication
about pills, or rubber insulation
about the many little infestations
so you relieve all your frustrations
now we have chronic overpopulation
and you cannot pay for sanitation
disease is rampant, across the nation
there's no money, for a childs inoculation
we need it all for a new space station

no condoms, you must resist the thrill
no abortions, Thou Shalt Not Kill
you should refrain, so God has willed
unless married, and your passion stilled
all those children, the fruit of evil
since Jesus didn't condone the pill
unwanted little children suffer, until
Us, not God, takes care of our own
If they live where our flag is flown
can we not take care of our own?

Wherever this flag is flown
it is spat on, burnt and stoned
this flag should not have gone
it should have stayed at home
taken care of just our own
our flag's reputation is blown
now we should care for our own

We send soldiers to burn their drugs
then buy the rest, because we're mugs
It costs more because we burn a lot
they don't care, we buy all they've got
those innocents we sent to fight
sleep in rags on the street tonight
all those we taught to fight and kill
are living with the nightmares still

Addicts, cripples, crazed and blind
search in vain for someone kind
we race ahead, leave them behind
we get the fruit, they chew the rind
come countrymen, is it not time?
that we all take care of our own
that we bring our flag back home
then whereever our flag is flown
we could take care of our own
we should take care of our own

Wherever this flag is flown
it is spat on, burnt and stoned
this flag should not have gone
it should have stayed at home
taken care of just our own
our flag's reputation is blown
now we should care for our own

TIDELINE

Where oceans tear with claws of foam
against the armoured cliffs of shore
The beach is strewn, when battle's done
with treasures from the ocean floor

In jumbled ruin seaweed lies
torn and battered on the strand
Feast for birds and crabs and flies
bounty for the skies and land

Moonlight brings ethereal scenes
luminous foam, along wavetops
Scientists ponder ways and means
but lovers pray it never stops

In rockpools under summer's sky
carapaced monsters run and hide
Cowering as we trample by
'til cool relief comes with the tide

The freezing blast of winters storm
moves on, some distant shore to flay
Bejewelled fantasy greets the dawn
with ruffles of lace in frozen spray

Our world, in sea-frets, is reborn
fantastic, ghostly forms abound
Familiar pathways now transform
breed monsters at the slightest sound

Our island home will always be
blessed by this beauty on all sides
Our wondering children born to see
their world transformed with every tide

TIGER TOES

Between the toes of a tiger
is a little soft patch of fluff
Stroke it and hear the tiger purr,
that is, if you're gentle enough!

The actual toes of a tiger
are sharp and terribly rough
As you will find out quickly
if you haven't been gentle enough!

Life is like a tiger's toes
it's nasty, cruel and tough
But now and then, unsuspected
there's love, if you're gentle enough

TIME OF COLOURS

Green, green, the world is green
a thousand shades, but all agleam
rippling waves, or tall and serene
thrusting, writhing, almost obscene
across the world an emerald sheen
the most verdant vista ever seen
of all the colours, this is the Queen
Green, green, the world is green

White, white, the world is white
don't know why, it came overnight
smoothing everything in sight
natures face in a state of fright
everything glows with ethereal light
a million diamonds sparkling bright
snowflake sculptures taking flight
White, white, everywhere white

Grey, grey, my whole world grey
all I knew just melted away
dare not move, nor dare I stay
recoiling, beckoning me to play
amorphous anonymity holds sway
imagination now running astray
mind is drifting, starts to fray
Damp and drifting, a world of grey

Gold, gold, everywhere gold
you thought you never would behold
enough to fill a treasure-ship hold
for a merchant prince or a pirate bold
bright and new, tarnished and old
autumn, gilded in wealth untold
overflowing each dip and fold
Gold, gold, all gleaming gold

Black, black, everything black
so confused, taken aback
one step astray, lost the track
moonbeam gleams upon storm wrack
a noise ahead, or behind my back
anticipating collision? attack?
praying for one lightning crack
Black, black, the night is black

Rubies, sapphires, and amethysts
across the meadow, through the mist
each petal a jewel on my list
A fairy princess dressed in bliss
would never gleam as bright as this
every dewdrop is rainbow kissed
all gathered now for some magical tryst
These gems, the colours I have missed

TOMMY AND HIS 303

When the Krauts came into Belgium clerks and gen'rals got to flee
Guess who they sent to 'old 'em? Tommy and 'is 303
They said we 'ad machine guns behind every tree and briar
But it was Tommy and 'is 303 and "5 rounds - rapid fire"

When all the clerks and gen'rals were back across the line
The word came down to Tommy to buy the Frogs some time
Now it's single shots an' pick yer man an' it's Tommy bleedin' now
But we made 'em bloody careful, though they came on any'ow

There's gay Paree be'ind us, an' in front of us the 'un
So now it's time to stand and 'old for Tommy and 'is gun
It comes to charge and counter-charge, and then the moment's passed
It were Tommy and 'is bayonet wot stopped 'em at the last

The cripples an' the blinded got to kiss a mam'oiselle
The rest of us got resupply and marched off into 'ell
Don't look for us in Vict'ry P'rades, marching with the band
They left Tommy and 'is 303 on the wire, in no-man's land

*For the professional British Army, out-gunned and outnumbered,
whose fighting withdrawal slowed the German advance
at the beginning of WWI.
Their lives were then thrown away
in frontal assaults on wire and machine guns*

TRANSFROGMIFICATION

A scruffy frog beside a pond, sat with a certain poise
Looked very strangely at me, made a weird Grrribgrrrit noise
I bent down to see more clearly, and nearly had a fit
The frog leapt forward suddenly and hit me on the lips!

It dropped down on the footpath, with the strangest sound I've heard
Rolled all around, legs in the air, then suddenly it blurrrred
Seemed to flow across the path, and then the little froggy
was suddenly a fairy large, somewhat tattered doggy
His fur was wet and matted, with pond weed here and there
He wagged his tail, shook his head and a fish fell out his ear

I thought this hasn't happened, or there was something in that tea
but it was worse, he coughed, and then began to speak to me
He said, "the magic wears off, so shut up while I explain
Did a whoopsy on the Wizard's lawn, I won't do that again
He enchanted me, made me a frog 'til kissed, a nasty trick
The word got out, a little girl found me and kissed me, quick
But when I stopped being a puppy, she wasn't quite so fond
Kissed me once again, and chucked me in the nearest pond
Little girls kiss young frogs, but won't kiss older ones
and the longer I've been froggy, the uglier I've become
You are no longer young and spry, but you looked right for me
I can no longer run and jump and stuff like that, you see
So I leapt in desperation, no-one so old would kiss a frog
but I'd seen you standing on your own, watching all those dogs"

We've been together years now, and I've found one thing is true
If you kiss your dog, to get him back, you will kiss a froggy too!

TRAVELLER'S TALES

Sit and marvel at traveller's tales
of distant places, not quite true
Ferocious tygers, dragons and whales,
encourage them with a pint or two

Or just once, step into the storm
Bare your face to the driving rain
Watch eagles play where lightning's born
Let wonder fill your heart again

TURNOVER

When each time we turn the calendar to the next month of the year
What happens to the pictures, I wonder are they truly here
Does the object of each picture wait, because we may come back
Or do they leave the scene, relax, cut themselves a little slack

Does the horse plod to his stables, to his oats and bed of straw
That pusscat head straight for her bed, in through her cat door
Does the blackbird fly back to her nest with worms to feed her brood
The fieldmouse leave the wheatfield, for a barn stuffed full of food

Will the eagle leave his posing perch, to look for careless rabbits
The fox, not so cute now, go back to his nefarious habits
Is squirrel off to leafy arbour, to find more yummy nuts to hide
Is the hound not quite so noble now, sprawled out before his fireside

Trout drifts in some limpid pool, ignores that tempting feathered fly
The otter dozes off, replete, too full to chase trout drifting by
Fishing boats return to harbour, the fisherman heads to the pub
The King of beasts looks silly, rolling around with all his cubs

Will that butterfly forgo her flower, to dance off on the breeze
The swirling cloud of starlings land, to roost in those convenient trees
The wolf and pups sleep in their den, safe from wind and rain
'til we turn the page, and they return, to pose for us again

UNIVERSAL INDIFFERENCE

I lit catherine wheels and rockets, a beacon for all the love in me
A blazing pyre of passion and loss, in a universe that cannot see

With exotic chemicals and spice, potent potions, fierce, intense
I strove for a flash of clarity, in a universe that makes no sense

I searched, enquired and studied ways that we were torn apart
But I found no road to reunion, in a universe without a heart

I uncovered cruel tortures, broken victims who cannot heal
Their pain made no impression, on a universe that cannot feel

I tried radio and radar, aimed technology at the sky
Asked the universe for direction, but there was no reply

I screamed, sobbed, and pleaded, howled the pain I cannot bear
A last despairing, fading cry, to a universe that doesn't care

Each horizon, East and West, fathoms deep, and the sky above
I searched every nook and cranny, but could find no place for love

VICTIM

Where is it now, that sparkle, that infectious love of life?
Effortlessly lighting up our lives, antidote to care and strife
The careless laugh, the innocent teasing, flirting charm
Safe among her family and friends, immune from harm

Delicate flower, plucked for careless pleasure, then thrown
to lie bruised and torn, abandoned, discarded and alone
Forever now, with that shadow always there behind her eyes
It tears my heart, a silent echo of her helpless, hopeless cries

Watch her stand apart, turning from the world to hide her pain
She cannot still that tiny voice, insisting she must be to blame
Reliving each awful moment, each word and step to violation
Re-visiting, looking for some misstep that invited his predation

Whatever punishment the beast one day may have to pay
No sentence will haunt his dreams, stalk him night and day
Where is her justice? No recompense can give her inner peace
We can only love her, and hope one day her nightmares cease

VICTORIOUS

Proud in our youth and strength, terrible to behold
We roam the land together, brothers fierce and bold
Sons of champions and heroes, born to fight and die
The greatest warriors ever seen beneath our Spanish sky

We strut and stamp, tear the ground, and bellow at the skies
A champion is needed. A chance to fight, to claim the prize
I am chosen! My moment come, my brothers stand, forlorn
For the chosen, the chance to sire the champions still unborn

The noise, the dust, confusion, but my brethren have been here
I smell their presence still - the sweat, the blood. The fear ??
The time has come, those voices are a raucous chanting row
I bellow to let them know, prepare! A warrior is coming now!

So where is my opponent? So much movement, all around
Horsemen pushing against me, confused, I give some ground
They are stabbing, jabbing, cutting, will not stand and fight
More wounds, more blood, where is the battle? It is my right

At last they cease. I stand, bloodied but not bowed
A jewelled little creature dances in, waves at the crowd
This is my opponent? This slight ephemeral flitting clown?
So be it. I charge across to smash him to the ground

He is gone! He skipped aside, he will not fight, just dance
This is no battle, he twists, evades, can only pose and prance
I caught him then! A stumble, the chance to strike is plain,
but confusion reigns, figures shout and wave, I miss again

He is cautious now, I have taught him to fear my blows,
But the spears flex in me, once more my lifeblood flows
I am failing, not defeated yet, but crippled and betrayed
It is coward blows that sap me now, not this warriors blade

He taunts me, one who has never bravely stood his ground
The crowd are jeering now, they see me slow, an ugly sound
The fool forgets just who I am, what proud lineage I hold
Postures, gesturing, there is one last chance if I am bold

At last I have the gadfly, dash him into the bloody dust -
but they will not let me at him! Coward! Run, then, if you must
For now I stand triumphant, wait for my prize, my heart's desire
Dreaming of fresh green pastures, of the sons that I will sire

Why do they come against me, with whip and horse and lance?
Drive me into this place of death, without a fighting chance?

Unbeaten, wounded and bloody, imprisoned by bars and chains
So dies their national emblem, the magnificent fighting bull of Spain

VISAGE

Though I have cried a million tears
since last I saw your face
All the tears in all the seas
could not that memory erase

Not all the patient labours
of the careworn thumb of time
Nor the sandstorms of eternity
can blur one hue or line

Now, as futures fade away
mortality holds no fear for me
For as I step into the dark
yours will be the face I see

THE VOICE OF SNOW

Across the meadow, fox-print, firm, determined, sudden pause
Hesitation, balletic leap, scattered grass, mark of nose and paws.
No sign of blood, this time the vole wins, cheats death again
Down vaulted alabaster halls he scampers, in their deadly game

Tic tac semaphore under the hedge, hesitation, under a bush
Slipping through the night, tangled maze, fraught with ambush
Risk the clearer way? Perhaps to catch bright, patient eyes,
Then unseen talons and cruel beak stoop from night skies

Crystal perfection, a clean, clear feathered fan is etched
Each pinion, each detail engraved, precise, sharp edged
The frozen memory of angels? Or pigeon bursting into flight?
Frantic, desperate lunge, blindly fleeing into protective night

Shattered 'neath the hammer blows of sunbeam and the breeze
Bright crystal razors drifting, scattering the subtle skill of freeze
While cowering in splendour, casting rainbows in the shade
Delicate extravagance lingers, the confections hoar frost made

WE KNOW BEST

You mustn't cut the forests down
the Earth needs them to breathe
With all the pollution going on
we need every tiny leaf

We'd like to help to save the trees
but there are none around
We needed fuel for factories
so we cut our woodlands down

You've managed very well so far
without cars and phones and such
You can't expect it all right now
the pollution is too much

We'd love to do our bit to help
our pollution ought to cease
But we can't ban cars and gadgetry
the voters wouldn't be pleased

WEAR IT WITH PRIDE

Stand tall, Dad, and wear it with pride
Let it all out, don't keep it trapped inside
You earned the right, with act and thought
With the lessons and example I was taught

The quarrels and the sleepless nights
This is your proof, Dad, you got it right
You see, I know you thought I didn't care
But I did, that's why you are standing there

You taught me to care about wrong and right
How, to keep us free, somebody has to fight
That someone has to hold, and not turn away
I held, Dad, and it brought you here, today

No politicians sons here, they don't fight
Mention it, when they ask for a sound byte
That smarmy geezer in his nice sharp suit
Ask if its the haircut, or don't they like boots

If Herself comes by though, it will be fine
She sent Her kin here too, to stand in line
Tell Her Maj no probs, that we all went willing
We knew the score when we took Her shilling

Broken hearted when they turned you away
When I volunteered, it really made your day
Marching in parades, as you longed to be
You have the right now, Dad, I paid the fee

Remember, Dad, no quaver when you speak
This day is for your warrior, not the meek
Stand up tall and straight, look 'em in the eye
Give the lads a show, Dad, as they march by

My Mum will ask, why should it be my son?
That's the thing, Dad, it shouldn't be anyone
But there is always some new foe to face
Which mothers son should die in my place?

I wish you could have taught a child of mine
Seems life's too short, there was never time
Tell your grandkids, Dad, 'ere they march away
to make a little time first, time to love and play

Stick that ribbon on Dad, go down the pub
Some won't like it much, and that's the rub
Stick out your chest, tell 'em to go to hell
I earned that ribbon, Dad, so you wear it well

As you sow, or so they say, so will you reap
I paid for your peaceful pint, and it wasn't cheap
Don't waste it all, Dad, on grief and acrimony
Live it full, Dad. If not for you, then live for me

WHAT WILL BE YOUR ANSWER?

What will be YOUR answer when the children start to pry?
Asking "were you on the battle-lines, or only standing by?
Were you marching for the Dolphin, fighting for the Butterfly?
What WERE you doing, Granpa, when the world began to die?"

From the future will they curse us, 'the folk from years gone by',
Who murdered all the creatures that crawl, or swim, or fly -
Who killed the flowers and the trees, and poisoned sea and sky,
Or will we start to understand, 'ere it's too late to try?

Will our children see the fire burning in the Tiger's eye?
Will they hear the Humpback singing, will they watch an Eagle fly?
Will they follow Badgers' footprints, really see a Crocodile cry?
Or will these just be legends, that WE allowed to die?

"There's plenty more fish" they always said, but I think you'll all agree
There's a lot less fish in the oceans now, than there really ought to be;
and they said that in the jungle, who would miss just one more tree,
But there's Ethiopian wastelands now, where a forest used to be!

When we learn that cans and bottles, bring death to Fox and Vole;
That our waste is still as deadly, when we put it in a hole;
and that smoke and sprays can poison the air from Pole to Pole;
Then we all will learn to save our piece - and together save the whole!

If we're going to save the forests, then we each must plant our tree,
stop saying what 'they' all should do, and say "its up to ME".
For we won't get rid of pollutants by flushing them out to sea,
and wrapping the World in plastic won't preserve the Ecology!

WINTER'S HOLIDAY

The Old Man sent out a knife on the breeze
and it cut to the heart of the greatest of trees.
The glories of summer, so vibrant and bold
Fell in crimson, silver, and nine shades of gold

The Geese brought tidings, riding the storm
All who could flee, went South to the warm
The Ermine and Hare aged a year every night
Their coats bespotted and streaked with white

The Hedgehog and Dormouse, Bee and the Bat
curled up in their homes, to sleep off their fat
Though Buzzard and Raven, Fox and the Crow
wait silent, impatient for death in the snow

Old Man strode down with frost at his heels
and ice rimed the windows, ponds and the fields
He laughed, and as his breath billowed around
Silent, relentless, snow smothered the ground

Then gusts and swirls, with a shriek and a roar
Shaking each branch, testing window and door
While pale in the moonlight, a river of foam
The shepherd is bringing his flock safely home

The Hunter races the storm and the night
His Hound just a fleck of Jet in the white
Lost and alone in the heart of the storm?
Why no, the old dog has brought him home

Soon ice rippled out to seal puddles and lakes
and the geese and the ducks crowded every break
The earth lay gripped in Winter's iron clasp
and Frost scattered diamonds on cobwebs and grass

The great fires were lit and great feasts were laid
Toasts were drunk and great speeches made
While close by the hearth sat the young and the old
and told stories of witches, goblins - and gold

But Old Man yearned for lands without trees
For bergs of glass set in icebound seas
For the freezing fire of the Northern Lights
where great bears roam the endless night

With emerald blades to carve the way
the Snowdrop checked that he'd gone away
So Crocus and Daffy, their bulbs unsealed
could paint with glory the woods and fields

All the trees and bushes sighed in relief
made intricate plans for blossom and leaf
The Old Man chuckled, chill tingled ears
He knew he'd be back again, next year

THE YUKON WOLF

(a work in progress, it will grow, as all tall tales do...)

I'll tell you a tale
of the Yukon Trail
where storms sweep out of the north
Where men with picks
swarm like ticks
and dig for all they're worth

The stories began
spread man to man
of a creature fierce and bold
Who emptied traps
chewed coonskin caps
and stole their arctic roll

So Twinkletoes Dave
who was fast and brave
said "I'll wear him down to a shadow"
His hounds set off
but soon enough
poor Mrs. Dave was a widow

McDonald felt
that under his kilt
was something to make a wolf fly
When Don mooned
the ladies swooned
Wolf cocked his leg in reply

But bearskin Pete
stamped his feet
swore no wolf was that tough
He took loads of traps
shotguns and maps
but came staggering back in the buff

Jock the Scot
claimed, after a tot
"my bagpipes will scare him away"
We all left town
can't stand the sound
of the Wolf as he learns to play

From dogcatcher Mitch's
Pierre took some bitches -
distraction, while he sneaked up
The bitches came back
with Pierre's backpack
now the town is infested with pups

Then Dandy Jim
so tall and slim
with a rifle that killed at a mile
Took seven mules
and a couple of fools
but he hasn't been seen for a while

'Enri the Walloon
said "wiz my balloon
I weel cut 'im off at ze pass"
In spring they found
a hole in the ground
and a bottle of laughing gas

Eskimo Nell
said "what the hell,
a wolf is a man with more hair"
She pouted and simpered
wiggled and whimpered
but all she attracted were bears

If you have heard further rumours about the Yukon Wolf,
please add them here...
and let me know!

PAWPRINTS

Its A Dog Thing 169
Pussy Angels 170
Pawprints On My Heart 171
Fireside Wolf 172
Calling Old Wolf 173
New Rules 174
First Present 176
The Shadow In The Corner 177
W M D 178
Breaking News 179

Just a few Samples

from

PAWPRINTS
ON MY
HEART

Poems about

Furballs and Dogbreath

from John Shillito

Published

2013

Available in

Hardback - Paperback - e-Book

ITS A DOG THING

tongues that slobber everywhere,
tousled, soggy, muddy hair

ears pricked up or flopping free,
tails that wag in ecstacy

cleaning out the cooking pot,
looking sorry when they're not

enjoying outdoors every season,
total devotion with no reason

leaping high with gleeful bound,
listening for the smallest sound

chase a ball, chase it again,
panting like a railway train

splashing into every brook,
mournful, "Didn't mean it" look

covering everyone in sand,
paws so gentle in your hand

gaze so soft and full of love,
rolling over for grooming glove

swimming in the roughest sea,
every moment full of glee

scrounging biscuits dipped in milk,
coat that gleams like oil on silk

welcome like a highland fling,
fur that sticks to everything

I've often looked, rarely found,
anything wondrous as a hound

PUSSY ANGELS

Yes, there are pussy angels, we're here, just out of sight
We look for lost, deserted souls, to soothe them in their fright

Those who die beloved, their souls are so serene and calm
As if some love came with them, protecting them from harm
But those you kill so thoughtlessly, their souls are torn and crushed
Broken, starved and murdered, betrayed by those they trust

We find them drowned in dirty bags, or crushed by callous boot
Starved in boxes in your dustbin, or tortured by some brute
Dumped carelessly in carrier bags, out in the cold and rain
Deserted, cowering in the pound, waiting for an end to pain

Tortured by your children, dumped at kennels when they scratch
Locked in cupboards, sheds and cages, buried in some nettle patch
You are lucky we are angels, and not as cruel as you
or we'd visit you in dreams, and you'd know pain and terror too !

PAWPRINTS ON MY HEART

Silken fur, soft and warm, slips smooth beneath my fingers
Long-gone now, but down the years, this memory always lingers
Whiskers on my cheek, wake me, startled, from my sleep
So many, many cherished moments, this one I will keep

Ping-pong balls, fish on strings, and a battered catnip mouse
Baby assassins honing skills spread laughter through my house
Feathers and leaves, mice and birds, a rat, maybe a rabbit
Trophy collection growing, until age and sloth erode the habit

Sun shines through uncounted pinpricks, riddling my lounge curtain
Where tiny paws, with tiny claws, learnt to climb, so uncertain
My favourite armchair, past its best, tattered and torn because
Mighty hunters prowl these halls, and find no trees to sharpen claws

On winter's nights, ferocious killer forgoes those ruthless ways
Curls up, kneading my poor knee, and there, contented, plays
A plaintive cry beside my bed, seeks shelter from the storm
Then cold wet fur, and ecstatic purr, curl up on someone warm

They gambol happily through my life, creatures of the wild, untamed
and in their careless, carefree wake, casual chaos reigns
But when, too soon, their span is done, each one as they depart
Leaves tiny scars upon my soul, and pawprints on my heart

FIRESIDE WOLF

There's a flicker behind those eyelids
as he sleeps in the fire glow
His tail flicks, his paws tremble
poised, he's ready to go
From between his teeth, an echo
of that ancient, haunting howl
as once more he hears the call
of his hidden, ancestral soul
He races over endless plains
back in the dawn of time
Pulls down his prey, now long-extinct
and calls the pack to dine

I rattle his lead. and he comes back
to modern, gentler habits,
He wags his tail, my fireside wolf
and we're off to annoy the rabbits

CALLING OLD WOLF

An Old Dog howling down the moon
We don't know what he is saying
Old white muzzle points moonward
but this time, Old Dog is praying

Old Dog calls out for Old Wolf
Hidden deep inside his soul
Calls him out for the Long Hunt
The long last run through dark and cold

He's telling Old Wolf time is short
of missing teeth, pains in his rear
of straining lungs and wobbly legs
He wants an end to pain and fear

Together now, they make their run
A last fast dash through endless night
An end to sorrow, fear and pain
his spirit gone by morning's light

You know he never meant to hurt
didn't leave, just went before
To wait, until you join the hunt
and he can run with you once more

Listen hard on moonlit nights
To the silence in the cold, clear air
Hear echoes of that ancient call
Know Old Dog still waits, somewhere

NEW RULES

Oh dear, Oh dear, I can't pretend it wasn't really me
Please don't shout or hit me, its a very tiny wee
Its all so very new and strange and very frightening too
There's noises, funny smells, and I'm not too sure of you

You were very kind and gentle when I met you at the Ark
But I felt very safe there, except for thunder, and the dark
When they left me in the evening, they put on my little light
I'm not sure that you will know that, you didn't visit me at night

You've got that hoover thing out, I must quickly run and hide
They used to stick it in my ears, said it was fun - they lied
You've put it down, said sorry, and really meant it too
Spoke softly, gave me treats, I'm sorry that I growled at you

Now this has got me so confused, not like it used to be
No shouts, no crowds, no other dogs, only you and me
I am being very quiet 'cos I don't want to make you cross
Though you seem to be quite peaceful, not like my other boss

I just can't help the tremble, now I've wee'd upon the mat
My hero!, you spoke to them, they stopped waving that big bat
And I knew I really should go out, but it was so very dark
So I messed on bed and carpet, at night I dare not bark

I tried to tell those ladies, and I'm trying to tell you
It's not your fault, I just can't help the awful things I do
You will never know the crimes committed in the park
Why I don't like my feet touched, flinch at every spark

The new rules in this house are very hard to understand
Its OK to lie on carpet, and no flinching from your hand
You have some funny habits, but the strangest one to me
is when we're watching telly and I'm allowed on the settee!

I'm trying to act better, to limit all this damage
I sometimes will relapse, its the best that I can manage
But if you promise that you'll keep me, that we will never part
I promise undivided loyalty, my love, and my battered heart

FIRST PRESENT

What's this, you've brought a present?
The first you've brought to me
How clever for such a little kit,
it's quite a big one, I can see

No, perhaps it's best left there
It's too sticky for my lap
and it's smelling quite obnoxious
How did you get it through the flap?

Even wiped a bit, I do not think
I will ever read that letter,
I'll use a tissue and move it all
There, back on the floor is better

Why yes, of course I'm very proud
of my ferocious hunting cat
I would prefer the next one fresher
Ah, I think its stained the mat

THE SHADOW IN THE CORNER

There's a rustle in the bushes but it's only the wind today
There's a ball and squeaky rabbit, but nobody wants to play
On the corner of my tea tray, two quarter-biscuits wait
and nobody tries to pinch those chips, at the edge of my dinner-plate

There's a dog-shaped hole in the doorway,
and the same-shaped hole in my heart
I just cannot accept it, and I don't know where to start
Because that shadow in the corner is too dark, and I can see
That when I come in through the doorway no-ones looking back at me

But deep within my sorrow, there's a tiny gleam of light
I have seen an old lost doggy, at the Ark, on their web site
When I look into those old, dark eyes, it really seems I see
He only needs someone to love him, needs it just as much as me

And now we both have been assessed, and so its time to meet
I'm going with a lot of hope, some worries, and a treat
I know he'll never be the same as that old friend of mine
But maybe we can make it work, with patience, and a little time....
:
:
:
:

My empty plate means life is once more as its meant to be
and from the shadow in the corner two brown eyes look back at me!

W M D

No scientist can figure out just how to turn it on
It leaves no operating marks, no trace when it has gone
They have looked for it with x-rays, the surgeon had to try
They know its there, know it works, but they can't figure why

I'm always very careful, only use it when I must
Don't want to overdo it, I don't want to lose your trust
Though I like to test it sometimes, I love to see it work
You seem to like it when I do, after all, it doesn't hurt

That disaster in the kitchen, its my fault, I must confess
You're waving both your arms about, I've made a real mess
There's not a lot that I can do, down here on the floor
I rub your legs, you pick me up, now I can go to war

I engage my secret weapon, just very faintly at the start
I don't hurry, wait a moment, 'till it penetrates your heart
Then gently stretch out on your lap, I know you like me there
Slowly increase the power, where your skin is touching fur

Thoughtlessly, you gently run your fingers down my back
So I push back against them, we seem to be on track
Bring the frequency up slowly, that's as high as it will go
Your blood pressure is dropping, your pulse is now quite slow

I can see you smile a little, as you slip into a trance
Against the secret power of purrr, you never had a chance
You are happy and relaxed, the annoyance melts away
my Weapon of Magical Distraction once more saves the day

BREAKING NEWS

The sky has just a hint of grey, one breath before the dawn
I hear a rattle from the catflap, then the touch of velvet paw
You tell me your adventures, where you have been tonight
The mysteries, the triumphs, how you had an awful fright

I listen to your meow and chirps, understand each gentle purr
Your fearless explorations, how brave you were out there
You tell of hunting mighty prey, of monsters in the dark
The sounds and scent of moonlight, and that awful, sudden, bark

I scratch behind your ears, stroke your slightly ruffled fur
My intrepid correspondent how I wish I had been there
Then the world bursts into life, serenades the first sunbeams,
and we slip down beneath the covers and drift quietly into dreams

A sort of Bonus

I Hope!

SHORT

STORIES

also by

John Shillito

Guns for the Ghost	*Gunrunners, Revolution, Lies and a Legend 'inspired' by mis-heard Lyrics in a song, Ghost*
Pyrate Dreams	*Fantasy comes and invades his Dreams, and Life*
The Heart of a Hunter	*A Hound's View of Fairness and Slavery*
Wolf and the Fast Food Bunny	*What does a young Wolf eat, when Mummy has been taken off by Social Services?*

One day, maybe,

they and their companions

might be published

in a book of stories

GUNS FOR THE GHOST

Inspired by misheard lyrics on Ella Henderson's 'Ghost'

The Sergeant cursed, but quietly because the lieutenant wasn't a man to annoy these days. He was one to take chances though, or maybe it was fear that had driven him to cross the river last night instead of waiting for dawn and the escort, fear of another failure. Now this. Behind him the men were busy loading the pack mules and clearing up the remains of breakfast, supervised by the corporal. That gave him an itch, a prickling of the hair on the back of his neck, the three of them together, for the first time since... He cut the thought short and looked around again, trying to pierce the gloom as the sky lightened a little. Not that it would help, he looked down to where he could barely see his own boots through the knee-high mist that had blanketed the hollow the squad had camped in, and the scrubland beyond. A clatter and a curse, he turned to see a dragoon picking up his rifle. Dragoons, they weren't even proper foot soldiers! Ten bloody raw recruits on horses, with just the three of them with any experience at all and some military genius sent them after the guns. No problem over the border where the foreigners had been happy to take the gold and turn over the long train of mules loaded with the new repeating rifles, the thousands of rounds of ammunition, the boxes of small, curiously patterned metal bombs, but if any trouble started now? Then again they weren't supposed to be here until the escort arrived, fifty veteran dragoons to see them across the river and the sixty miles to the fort. He looked around again, the two supposedly on guard were doing the same but even if the sky might have lightened a little there could be an army under the mist. Or...

"Give us the guns." He stiffened, it was a young woman's voice! Surely not, this was a thousand miles away?

"Give us the guns. Give us the guns." It was a low chant from the mist, light, almost melodic young women's voices but there was a deadly undercurrent.

"And the horses, maybe." This one was a little deeper, it had to be her! Solid voice for a Ghost, some inane part of his mind said as he looked back and forth, trying to catch any sign whatsoever of how many, or where. An exclamation followed by a dull wet smack and he turned to see the guard crumple with, with an arrow in him? A low moan from one of the recruits and he went to his knees as he caught sight of the metal vanes, white with ragged red crosses. Crossbow, the sergeant tried again to pierce the mist, but there was no noise, no movement under the gently undulating white blanket.

There was a clatter behind him, and a low moan followed by a sob. "It's them, it's them. Los Angeles. She is here, The Madonna, the Ghost of the Madonna. We're all dead." The recruit was rocking back and forth with his head in his hands. "I didn't do it, I wasn't there. I swear."

"Shut up or I'll shoot you myself!" The lieutenant turned, pulling his pistol and three pale, robed figures rose from the mist and dragged him down, there was a muffled noise and then silence. The sergeant had his rifle half up, but there was nothing to shoot at. It he fired blind he might hit the lieutenant, though that might be a blessing the little voice in his head told him.

"Give us the guns. Give us the guns." A little louder, more insistent.

The corporal laughed, a short, harsh noise. "May as well, at least it'll be quick." He flipped the bolt and the brass caught the sun as it flew out, then he threw his rifle down, and started to unbuckle his gun belt. He looked over at the sergeant, "it's been a long time coming, Corp." The sergeant started to move, to argue, to stop him, and then he felt the kiss of steel on his skin. On the inside of his thigh, the point was through the cloth right over the big artery, as a knife fighter the sergeant knew just what his chances were if he didn't keep very, very still, he'd bleed out in three steps. Distracted for just one moment and it was all over, after all the years of throwing sixes his luck had run out. Carefully putting his hand holding the rifle out to one side, the sergeant let it slide through his grip until the butt hit the ground and gave the weapon a little push. No point in shooting himself if it went off. Then he slowly bent forward and looked down. A pair of eyes looked back and with a jolt he recognised the hate and rage, but these were brown, not grey, and the hair showing from beneath the hood was thick and dark, almost black, not cropped short and copper coloured. The hood and robe were the same but there was no blood on them, or at least not unless he moved that little voice pointed out.

The recruits were throwing away their guns now and the sergeant winced but none went off. It might have been better if they had, the escort might be in earshot having a leisurely breakfast before heading for the river where he should be stood on the other bank, waiting. Stupid bloody recruits probably didn't even have one up the spout, five years of fighting bandits and rebels taught you to do that if you lived long enough. Many more robed figures were rising from the mists now, had they recruited a bloody nunnery, a convent? The crossbows here and there were held steady though, no fluttery little virgins among this lot and the sergeant wondered for a moment if it might be quicker to move now and get a clean death, in case he was a special case. Though it hadn't been him. You didn't stop it though, and your soul is just as black that inconvenient voice reminded him. The women parted silently and a figure moved forward, towards him, the light wasn't quite enough to see her face but the robe with the jagged, stained slash across the belly, the faded hand prints and the dark splash at the throat was enough. A bolt of superstitious dread went through him. The Ghost! Although his rational mind said she wasn't dead, yet he had seen her die himself! Then he was near enough to see the eyes, those same grey eyes but steady, considering, weighing his worth, judging his guilt, and a great calm came over him. He reached for his belt. She stood silent as he removed his helmet, bandoleer, and finally his boots and knelt before her, then she looked deep into his eyes.

"Do you seek forgiveness, sinner?"

"I do, Madonna." And, he realised, he truly did, despite swearing he never would. His mind was suddenly back there, that dusty, nameless village with adobe huts and the church, doors smashed and laid in the street. He had finished with the woman and passed her to one of the men and now he wanted loot, or maybe a bit of wine if the pigs hadn't already drunk it. It was almost gone, just as he was about to tell the idiots at the altar to save some for him there was a short, quiet cry from the small door at the side, and he wandered over and opened it. Two bandaged rebels on rough pallets with their bellies and throats wide open and still bleeding. A hairy pale arse under a blue tunic up between between two paler, smoother legs, a pair of rough knickers with a bloody hand print still hung from one ankle. Over the soldier's shoulders a pair of grey eyes looked back, alive with rage and hate under the close cropped copper hair and he realised, with a shock, she was a nun. "Piss off will you, or I won't be done before she dies." The voice was strained, but if he was up to his balls in a young virgin there was no wonder.

"I'll take seconds from that!" The corporal moved a little to the side, enough to see the broad slash across the belly, the dark gleam of intestines. "Christus!" He had some stomach, to screw that! "Remember to cut her throat" as he backed out and shut the door, then headed for the wine. The silly shits were wasting it by pouring some into the open mouth of the priest, spread-eagled over his own altar with the jagged end of the wooden cross driven into his chest. "Oi, give me some of that." He needed to wash that sight away or he'd not be able to get up his next woman. It all went through his mind in a moment, and those same eyes were looking at him now as the Ghost spoke again.

"I am not the Madonna, I am but a ghost. If you wish to ask her for forgiveness, so be it. Open your mouth."

The sergeant opened his mouth and felt the little wafer on his tongue, and as he raised his head to drink the mouthful of wine he felt the warm sun on his skin, and the wetness of the tears running down his lined, scarred, stubbled cheeks....

"Why? The lieutenant had his helmet off, scratching his head as he looked at the line of soldiers in their bare feet, laid in crumpled heaps with a pool of dark red drying blood beneath each throat. The stink of shit and the sharp tang of blood in the air were familiar, but there had been no fierce, bitter conflict first. "They didn't even fight except the guard there, and he didn't actually fight, he just didn't get the chance to surrender. No rope marks, no bruising. They stripped down and knelt to have their throats cut!"

"But they were forgiven first." The general was too old to be out in the field, too senior to be commanding fifty men but the Jefe had been adamant. He wanted those guns safely back in the armoury before anyone else knew they were in the country. "Look in their mouths, there'll be a wafer and it'll be wet with wine. They knelt to be forgiven, it's the Ghost." The nearby troopers crossed themselves or kissed their crucifixes. Then looked guilty. The general sighed, "maybe it's over, these were the last three. It's why they had recruits, nobody else would serve with them. In case she came to find them."

"Who? Which three? I suppose the lieutenant was one, he had to be one." The trooper who'd found the body had lost his breakfast, as had two of those burying the remains and the lieutenant wasn't feeling too good. "But the rest all went easily by comparison, and it still doesn't make sense."

"No it doesn't. We had a survivor just over a year ago, wounded and trapped in the rubble and he kept quiet and they missed him. She turned up and asked who wanted forgiveness, with the bloody great slash across her belly and a cut throat, he swore it. All the prisoners knelt and she said they couldn't be forgiven as soldiers, so," the general waved at the neat row of bare footed bodies. "Belts, bandoleers, helmets and boots, it's what we give a recruit to make him a soldier. Then she went down the row and gave each one forgiveness, a wafer, and a drop of wine, and when they lifted their heads to drink the wine she cut their throats. Fifty four of them and not one ran, or fought, and the last ones had to know what was coming. She's got a big crucifix on a chain round her neck, it's got a blade in it, like a sword-stick."

"A dead nun? How many dead nuns have there been? Hundreds, so what was so special about this one? Anyway, she can't be dead if she's cutting throats!"

"Ah, you've been away, it's probably why you got this job, we have too many deserters who want to ask forgiveness before she comes for them and one of them would have told her if they'd got the job. Somebody did anyway. It was why those three got the job, because everyone knew they wouldn't run off to tell her." The general took a moment, not many people didn't know some version of this already. "It was the usual, a village sheltering rebels so they all died, but not before the men had some fun. Looting, rape, the usual, but this time someone raped a nun." He raised his hand, "yes, not the first, but it was a nasty one, he'd opened her gut first and did her while she was dying, and some say she cursed him and every soldier in the army." The general looked round, then over at the single barefooted figure slumped separately. "He was the corporal at the time, don't know why he surrendered or why she didn't treat him the same as the lieutenant, who was a sergeant at the time and in charge of the whole mess."

"Maybe she forgave him. Perhaps he was truly sorry?"

"Thank you sergeant, just what we need. Tell the lads that if they're sorry they'll get a nice clean cut throat instead of" he waved a hand towards the hump over the lieutenant.

"Sorry sir." The sergeant waved a hand, "it's just..."

"So who did it, or did she already get him? No, that's crap, she can't be a real ghost!" The lieutenant glanced around, "how many actually believe all this?"

"Easier to count those who are sure it isn't true. At least half the rebels and bandits in the country claim to fight for her now and most of our rank and file will shit themselves if she turns up. The rest of us? I wish I could disbelieve, but you've seen this and there are dozens of reports of places like this. Lines of bodies." He spat into the dust. "Bad as the lieutenant is, I'd save a prayer for the corporal, he was a trooper then, it was his first fight."

"And?"

"He was the rapist, and they've taken him." The general shuddered briefly. "They played with the lieutenant long enough, I hope the men were dead first because I'd hate to think they knelt and listened." A scout came back on foot and shook his head.

"Lost them sir. The tracks go off towards the badlands, into the broken ground and the whole lot either went up one of the ravines or split all over the place. We'd need everyone to look further, and it would be expensive?"

"How expensive?"

"My horse is back there. Crossbow from among the rocks and I wasn't even looking at sign. I was stood scratching my head, next to the horse, and down it went. It was a warning I think." He carefully showed the general a broken stub, white flights with jagged red X, then hid it from the men again. "Los Angeles, they know these badlands." The scout was right, fifty men who would have to leave their horses to go into that lot, against fighters who knew every inch of it. Expensive summed it up.

"So we let them go?" The lieutenant had definitely been abroad, not fighting rebels through the scrub and rocks.

"You suggest we let them kill another fifty and collect their rifles as well, as a bonus?"

"A bonus? They only got a dozen."

"You may as well know, everyone will need to. We are here, in this godforsaken arse end of creation, because our neighbours have been good enough to sell us some of those new repeating rifles of theirs. Or someone stole them and was willing to sell, though a thousand are a lot to steal."

"A thousand? We've only got ten of those here between fifty men! How much did that cost?"

"Enough so that you might want to hang onto your last pay, the next could be late."

"But even if they got the gold, will a foreign government sell to rebels?"

"Too late, because this misbegotten, cretinous excuse," the general waved at the hump of earth "was supposed to stay across the river until we arrived. Since the rebels have been very careful not to cross the border and upset anyone and he already had the bloody guns!" The lieutenant paled, and stared, aghast. Heads turned nearby at the raised voice but the general was past caring much. "With fifty thousand rounds of ammunition and four hundred of the new hand bombs." The general ignored the quiet muttering as the word went round the men, he was remembering the last thing the Jefe had said. 'With these guns we can finish this war'. With those guns the Ghost might finish the war, and not in a way the general could survive. Already he was wondering if there was a way to get his wife and family clear, with enough gold to give them a life somewhere. One bloody woman, why couldn't the randy little shit have kept it in his pants, or used one of the village women since they were all killed anyway.

The town was quiet now, the explosions, then the shooting and screaming and later the single gunshots and fireworks as the men, and women, celebrated. He had survived! Louis laid back on his bed, a real bed, and dozed. Seven months of following his Ghost from battle to ambush to desperate rearguard to savage assault, and he had lived! So many of those young robed figures laid in fields and ditches but there were always more, and more of the pale, frightened deserters begging for forgiveness and asking if they could earn redemption. She should have died a dozen times at least, that brought a wry smile, the Ghost couldn't die according to most of her own fighters and all the enemy, she was already dead. He had seen her, time after time, seen the opposing ranks falter and run or fall to their knees when that stained robe led the assault. She hadn't spoken to him since those few words, and now he would probably never see her again.

There was a noise at the door, and a robed figure came in and looked round. "Only me in here." Because he couldn't, though some of the women had tried. She picked up his gun and gunbelt, boots and helmet, and left without a word, leaving a figure in a torn robe in the doorway. Louis came upright, heart in mouth. He had wondered, but now? He knelt. "Is it time?"

"It is." She came inside and closed the door, then threw the hood back and he gasped, he couldn't help it. This was the face of his dreams, his nightmares, but the rich copper hair was down to her shoulders now, and though the face was a little older, a little weather beaten, and there were worry lines here and there, she was still beautiful. His mind was flipping back, comparing, seeing her laid on the vestry floor looking up. He had burst in and bayoneted the two wounded men as they struggled to rise, and then there she was, knelt, looking calmly back at him as she prayed. He could hear the men crashing through the church and the voice of the priest raised in protest, then outrage, and then a short, pained cry. They would be in here soon and he just couldn't. He couldn't do it.

Frantically he had looked around but there was nowhere to hide, and she smiled, very slightly, and then he knew what had to be done. Her eyes went wide as he threw her onto the floor, then she whimpered in shock as he slashed the bodies open. She braced, resigned as the bayonet came for her but he cut through the robe, not flesh. Maybe not flesh. He snatched pants from the scattered clothes by the corpses and threw the bloody blanket back over, but when he pulled up her robe she started to struggle, giving a short cry. Bugger, Louis hung the pants round one ankle and put a bloody finger to her lips, then grabbed a handful of intestines and dumped them into her robe, covering the pale flesh beneath. He barely got his pants down and dragged her legs around him before the door opened and the corporal's voice came over his shoulder. That was when her eyes came alive with hate, when he did nothing but ask for seconds. Louis often wondered why the corporal hadn't heard the strain in his voice, he had those soft thighs in his hands and was only too aware of the heat of her groin on his, even through her underclothes, and she must have felt it. The hate in her eyes died down a bit when the corporal left and he had arranged her, sprawled to show the slash and intestines and one thigh smeared in blood, with a hand across her face and a pool of blood under her throat. He'd thought it was all for nothing when the sergeant, later the lieutenant, had told them to burn the place. Louis had suggested leaving it so the peasants and priests could see the cost of sheltering rebels and the sergeant had agreed, though he sent men around to check everyone was dead. Word of the raped and murdered nun spread among the men, and the corporal had added the details, and at first he was notorious. Later he was hated, feared, and blamed for the rise of the Ghost, a rise that began that night when a sentry was found dead. It was several bodies later when someone found the wafer and wine in a mouth, he was looking for gold fillings, and soon word spread of people seeing a dead nun with her belly wide open and bloody hand prints on her robes. One general was known to have suggested shooting Louis and sending her the body, men began to avoid him and soon he could only be posted with new recruits. As soon as they learned who he was the stares would come, and the itchy feeling between his shoulder blades.

Then the Ghost had found him, he lifted his head for the knife and instead she said "follow me" and he was given his boots back. A day later he was given a uniform, and then later a gun, and he was put into the line. Now Louis was commanding a company of irregulars, bandits with a cause, and in all that time he had never spoken to her, never seen her face again. His soldiers knew who he was, they called him 'the sinner', 'the redeemed' or 'the forgiven' behind his back, and fought like maniacs because they fought for their own redemption, believing that they would also be forgiven for their sins if they died fighting for the Ghost. Knowing that the man who led them had been one of the enemy and the worst of them all, that he had killed and raped and looted his way across the country with the army but been forgiven. Now here she was, smiling slightly as if she could read the thoughts tumbling through his head and he knew his own release was at hand, because he deserved it, because he was a murderer and looter. Though not rapist because he had never had a woman, willing or not. He always saw her face and the desire died.

Angelica wasn't smiling at the young man sat on the bed, she was trying to sort out the turmoil in her own head. She was wondering who should be asking for forgiveness from who. The Sinner who was innocent or the Ghost with bloody hands. When the corporal had come in and wanted to join in the rape he thought he saw, for the first time she felt true hatred. It settled deep inside her and burned into her soul as she laid in the blood of her patients, while she listened to the screams outside stop, one after another. While the men came checking, kicking some of the bodies but not hers because they saw the intestines, the underclothes and the bloody hand prints on her legs and robes as he had arranged her. Settled and burned until it turned into an insatiable lust for vengeance, a need to seek repayment for all those raped and murdered innocents. Now there was an aching void inside, crying to be filled because what do you do after you have had your revenge? If your revenge involves years of unrelenting hate and the death of thousands, the tearing apart of a whole nation to hunt down forty men, what happens afterwards, how do you become something else if hate is all you are?

She had intended to kill this man when she found him, the whole legend was based on his supposed sin and the legend was winning a war. Then he had looked up at her, and she remembered him looking down, ashamed of the reaction of his groin and terrified that the corporal would realise the truth, and something melted. A little bit of the hate faded and she kept him alive as her own chance of salvation, a small gesture for the thousands of men and women she sent to die, joyfully, in the name of her vengeance. Instead the Ghost had sent him out to die at another's hand and created another legend. The Sinner Redeemed, who led an army of the damned to earn his redemption, who could not die because he had already passed through that gate, who came to gather the blackest of souls into his band. A man who had looked for his death and had led his mob of bandits into battle time after time, seeking his final reckoning. It had never come and now she found that she was happy that it hadn't.

Louis looked up as she took off the cross and pulled out the blade, then he closed his eyes and lifted his chin for the knife. Instead he felt a soft brush of skin on his lips, a kiss? His eyes flew open to see her straightening, a faint smile on her lips. "I have never done that before."

"But you? You're a nun!"

"No, never a nun and I have felt too much hate, shed too much blood to ever be welcomed back to the church. The innocent novice died and became something else, the Ghost, and now everyone fears my hatred." The knife went up for her throat. "It is time for peace, for forgiveness, and so the Ghost must die." His hand went up in protest but the blade cut the worn cloth instead of the soft flesh, and she slipped the robe off her shoulders to fall on the floor. His eyes went to the thin white line on her belly and then back up to see the smile blossom. "Perhaps it is time for Angelica to live."

— 192 —

PYRATE DREAMS

I have to write this all down now. Already fact and rumour are spreading and mixing, and soon there will be few who can remember how it all started. Most people have only seen clips, the bits a particular news channel found the most interesting, or titillating. Maybe, in the end, nobody will care. I can remember every detail, I wish I could forget. Just for a while. Drugs and alcohol don't work, even in their oblivion I dream.

Such an innocent start. As everybody knows except the few people on the planet who never even talk to someone with a newspaper, phone or the TV, it was a big Film Premiere. The Pirate thing, which might be why they chose it. I was a real fan, of the star (female of course) and from the pre-release clips, it was a real bodice-ripper. I know, but at 20, sound of mind and body and without a girlfriend, a man can dream. So I went early, got a place on the rails, and settled down for a fleeting glimpse of the object of my passions. My wildest fantasy was an autograph on an A4 poster. Fantasy, hell, I really didn't know what a fantasy was. Now I do, and so does most of the population, and fantasy is not all it was supposed to be.

That was the thing, no one was worried, nobody thought it was strange. Most were enjoying the show, thinking it was a bit of an extra, a fancy stunt for the assembled media to plug the product. Most people left still believing that, but I got too close. We were a good crowd, it was a fine evening, and the road was closed for the great and good to arrive by limo and strut their stuff. We thought most had gone, and I had a couple of (slightly disappointing) photos of my dream girl - that is a phrase with a different meaning now! She looked a little older, a bit skinnier than in my version of reality, but that seems to be the norm with actresses. Everyone was chatting to each other in the crowd, the last few B-listers were working up the carpet, and a bell rang. Not a door buzzer, it was one of those ship bells you hear on films. Loud but mellow, and it echoed, right down in your bones. Then instead of a limo, this cross between a motorised rickshaw and a pirate ship eased into the kerb. I just wrote that, it sounds stupid, and I can't find a better description!

Then again, most of you must have seen it. All the footage that was broadcast in those first few moments and was recorded elsewhere. Before it all went tits-up..

First to catch the eye was the rider. She sat on the front like a real biker chick, all tight leather and attitude, steering the damn thing into the kerb. When she started to uncoil, it got the attention of every man there! Then all hell broke loose. I had my phone up to get a picture (me and everyone else) when it went blank. Suppose its all old news now, but that blackout thing was a real shock up close and personal. My phone just died. Then a lot of muttering as everyone else started shaking their phones and cameras, or bashing buttons. There was a lot of action from the TV crews, except we didn't notice straight away, what with us all swearing at our own bit of misbehaving technology. Some of us noticed the TV lot when we looked round to see who else had lost service, and saw the serious types at the door poking and prodding ears and lapels and muttering to each other. It was the radios going down of course.

We have all heard the theories now, but not a single one that makes sense. Localised intense EMP was the nearest that gives an idea of the effect. Except later it turned out EMP hardened equipment went down as fast as my phone. They have never found a transmitter, and the effect persisted, killing electrics long after they left. There were bods in white suits buzzing around the area as soon as us plebs were out of there, and one of the papers reported some slight lessening just recently, but don't take your phone anywhere near the place if you want it functional. Anyway, that was all later, and you have all seen the barriers on TV and heard the scientists and talking heads waffle on about it for hours by now. So, all the electrics died, and a sort of mutter started up, and, most of us simply forgot about the weird limo and the biker chick.

It took a loud crack to get us all focussed again. Some ducked, and quite a few types in suits stuck their hands inside jackets, but it wasn't a shot. It was the biker chick, and she was stood there with an honest to god whip in her hand. Well it worked, it got everyone's attention, and when she was sure she'd got our attention, she made sure she kept it! That suit was NOT leather, and if I hadn't seen it come off, I would have sworn she was sewn into it, or painted it on. And boy, did she know it. She stretched to make sure the boys hadn't missed anything, then reached up and peeled off her helmet. It was no disappointment - classic Brit aristocracy beauty, tall with all the right bumps and curves, and a mane of deep red hair halfway down her back. I mean, wow, she had a whole fan club there and then, even if the whole thing looked choreographed. She called something that no-one then or since can work out, a sharp barking command, and the whole show got on the road.

First, two more gorgeous women stepped down from the back of the trike-whatever, dressed in a porn directors version of a pirate costume. Just a long jacket really, very fancy with ruffles and laces, based on the dress coats you see in Trafalga-era movies. Of course, if it is cut low, and is high enough to show the fancy tops of their stockings, and only held by a few loops which don't quite close the front, the actual impression is somewhat different. Add a pair of high, and high-heeled boots, a sword on a sash across the chest, and a pistol and neatly coiled whip, and HM Navy would definitely not have approved. The sailors would, as did the crowd, they were greeted by several wolf-whistles which they totally ignored. Instead one of them pulled on a thin chain, and out came the eye candy for the girls. Blond, long hair in a leather band, three-quarter length tight leather pants, and Doc Marts. The rest was oiled, bronzed muscle. There were a few very feminine wolf-whistles, and the ladies started to pay more attention. That bloke had muscle where I don't even have rumours of muscle, and I am no 10 stone weakling. He stood very straight and proud but he surely didn't argue much, and the collar attached to the chain settled where he stood in the hierarchy. He didn't have any weaponry either, but he didn't look as if he needed much. He was in turn holding a couple of leashes, and at least there were animals on those.

My first thought was what the hell? I thought it was illegal to domesticate wolves. They were NOT German Shepherds, I've had those. These were the rough relatives the GSDs don't talk about. Male and female, they didn't really look huge until they moved far enough to get a scale from the barriers, if they were part wolf, the rest was pony. A black male, and a white bitch. A lot of this detail only comes from re-running it in my head, later. The overall impression at the time was entrancing. They played us, and we all just went with it, going oooh and aaah in the right places.

The other 'Porn Pirate' came round the front to the driver with another bronzed adonis, this one was black haired and carrying an armful of clothes. The redhead (the other two were blonde and raven haired, almost matched the dogs) still facing the crowd, peeled open the Velcro or whatever seam down the front of her suit, which extended down the inside of the legs, and dropped it to the floor. I wonder how many women winced when that luxurious creation hit the dirt? None of the men were looking at the suit, believe me. She stood there without the slightest hint that she wasn't in a private dressing room, the exact opposite of sexy. Oh, she was a centrefold fantasy in red lingerie, with an underbra made legal by a ruff of lace, a pair of pants like hot pants but looser and silk (my uncle says they are French Knickers, but he didn't actually see them so who knows..?), a pair of those boots, and those stockings that don't need suspenders to stay up. About now I could have done with some help to stay upright - and breath. Be fair, I am human, and I came here to see a sexy lady. OK, I got more than I bargained for, but its not my fault. Anyway, she holds out her arms and the adonis slides on a soldier/sailor top like the other two, but hers was white with red frogging (I looked it up, its the name for the fancy bits on the front). And yes, the two with red coats had white stockings, and presumably white underwear. Well, definitely white, actually, but that's getting ahead. I've got enough problems concentrating without getting out of sync. That white underwear does my head in. To be honest the white was more ivory, like the old dresses and stuff in the museum, but it still does my head in.

Must hurry and get this all down, and put it somewhere to be found. Hide it? But not too well. Don't even know if someone will look, its all getting a bit crazy. The usual services are not being resumed. It is so hard to concentrate, I don't think it will be too long now. Either that or I will lose it altogether and go looking, but my pride still stops me from going that far, the last dregs of resistance. Even if someone believes it, perhaps it is too late to help, if anything ever could have helped.

Anyway, she slides into her porn outfit, nice and slow, and adjusts the sash and gun belt (if she'd asked for help, a lot of people would have died in the rush), carefully coils the whip, and then looks up. The whole crowd was silent. I really don't know what we expected, but every face was concentrating on her, and she just looked right through us all, and snapped her fingers.

The door on the side of the 'cabin' bit swung slowly up, and like Pavlov's dogs, we all swivelled to look. Inside were three people, and a lot of silk and cushions and such. The centre character was a man. A big man. Not fat, but no brick wall would fancy running into him. Clean shaven, hair back in a queue (looked that up too) with a gold clasp. Looked a well-preserved mid-thirties, but who knows? He was lounging back wearing the male version of the jacket, in white silk with gold frogging, and (thank God) leather trousers and floppy-top pirate boots. He smiled a little, and shooed his two companions to the door. They quickly shuffled out (actually they oozed out with a supple grace that looked way easier than it could have been) and placed a step outside the door for His Lordship. As you all now know, he is actually known as the Master, but allow me a bit of a dig. Compensation for feeling so bloody inadequate.

It was the boys' turn again, like a roller coaster. Wind up the lads, calm down the ladies, eye candy for the girls, let the blokes take a breath. Well, I was definitely short of breath by now. His two companions were presumably the female equivalent of the adonis twins, and while they didn't have quite the same impact for me as the strip queen there was plenty of appreciative comment. Blonde and Brunette again, oriental and viking. One with a little veil and a sheer gown that would have given an imam a heart attack, plastering against the skin where it touched, and the other in (not many) bits of fur, including little boots. Both had the collars, gold ones, but their chains were hooked to gold chain belts at the waist. When he came down the step, they knelt, one at each side, and held up his sash, sword, and gun belt. He did the arms-out bit, and they arranged the weaponry, but then they both looked very expectantly at him. He debated for a second, then looked at Gudrund the Viking goddess (well, I have to call them something) and nodded. She ducked back in and appeared with this bloody whip. It was a beaut. The handle was, presumably highly illegal ivory, nicely carved with a leather grip, and the rest was braided leather about 12 ft long. We know, because he gave it a quick crack, scared the shit out of me and one of the security blokes told me two of them had their guns half out. He grinned, the bastard, then slowly coiled it and put up his hand under Gudrund's chin. She jerked away, obviously niggled, and he said something to her that made her hang her head. The next bit was either some strange scripting, or as I have come to believe, just plain weird. He put the handle of the whip under her chin, and she *went still. She was already not moving, but she froze, completely, not a muscle twitching. Then he slowly lifted her head with the whip until she was looking into his eyes. Not a flicker, no defiance, no anger, if anything she looked almost pleading. Then he lowered the whip, still in contact with her skin, down the front of her neck, between her breasts, and down her belly. To my inexperienced eye, she looked as if she was about to faint, but when I described it, my uncle swears she was having an orgasm, and with his reputation I believe he would know. Himself (Master, not my uncle) stopped at the belt, and everyone in the crowd started breathing again, if a little heavily. I don't know what we thought he was going to do, and no one wanted to tell what they were expecting. He unhooked the chain and turned to collect the chain from Miss Saigon, and Gudrund actually swayed and closed her eyes.*

Then suddenly every one was lined up and set off along the red carpet. No punch line, that really threw me, and a lot of others. I was waiting for an advert for a film, some plug for an actor (a plug for the local house of ill repute?), but they just started for the door. It wasn't boring, though. For starters, a flock of security bods and those meet-and-greeters came shuffling down to meet them. It was obvious they had no idea what to do, and it started to dawn on a few of us that all was not right. The Strip Queen was out front, sword on her shoulder, then two porno soldiers (African-Jamaican? Who knows when they popped out or where from?). His Lordship next with his 'slaves' tripping along a step behind, then Adonis I and II with their puppies. Last came the original two porno soldiers, with their swords on their shoulders. It was dead impressive, there was a hell of a lot of fine flesh being very well displayed, and the whole circus rolled forward with no hint of any intention of stopping, so the greeters had a problem. It got a little more serious when one of the security bods put a hand out to stop the Porno Queen. To be fair he spoke first, and tried to put a hand on her shoulder, but she straight-armed him onto his back and the sword point was on his neck in a flash. From the way he froze, it was sharp. That bloke was about 14 stone and went down like a sack of rocks. The other security blokes were prodding their ears and lapels trying to talk to someone, and the greeters scattered like chickens faced by an eagle. Some hands went into jacket fronts, the Afro porno pair (I wish I knew someone's bloody name) pulled out Dick Turpin pistols (which, as we found out later, work much better than the originals) and brought the swords off their shoulders, and those of us with a brain started to pull back from the barriers. Then the Master put in his six pennorth. Don't know what he said to the Porno Queen, no-one can figure out the language, let alone translate any of it, but she backed up a quarter inch and raised the sword. Whereupon Mr. Embarrassed shuffled back and stood up, looking daggers, which was wasted because I don't think it would have fazed her if he'd thrown real ones. You can get the names for the guards and such from the records, but I don't care enough. Then The Master crooks his finger and, after a quick no-you-go one of the greeters was shoved forward to meet him. All the weaponry except Porno Queen's sword was safely stowed away and that was back over her shoulder. Not that anyone who had seen how fast she got it into action would consider that any comfort. Given the look on her face now I wouldn't have tried anything if she had been tied up and even more nearly naked!

It is dark now. The electric is off again, but who knows if it is because of them or just the workers at the power station staying at home. There is a lot of that about now, and it is spreading. I hate reading and writing by candlelight, but batteries are like unicorn droppings these days. Hoarders, or just panic? Where are we. Oh, yes, nearly there. I don't want to really think about it, but I didn't speak up at the time. It may not have helped, it may not help now, but I want to tell someone, and it is too late to talk to someone. I don't want anyone here when it happens. It makes me sweat just thinking about some other poor bastard being here. I think it's because I am worried about what might happen to them, but at least it's partly because they might interfere. Because a part of me wants to be on my own. With her.

So this poor woman eases past the advance guard veeery carefully, sticks on her professional smile (full marks for that, I would have been looking for a change of underwear) and stops in front of him. He stuck his hand out to the side, which made the poor bitch flinch, and one of the rearguard collected the chains for his pets. Then he stepped forward, leaned closer, and said something very quietly in her ear. That was definitely a look of relief that appeared, and she nodded and swiftly exited towards the main doors. Then we all stood there. At least to start with. The Master stuck his hand out again and the Blonde handed him the leashes, then turned to go back. And stopped. She was looking straight at me! At the time several of us thought we were the object of attention, and I did look behind me, but it soon became obvious I was the lucky boy! Instead of getting back into line, she started to sashay - nothing else describes that movement, believe me - over towards the barrier. No one else was moving, so attention swung towards her, and me. It was like a bloody tennis match, heads moving back and forth to follow the action. Well, apparently I was the action. She stopped a few feet away and gave me a slow up-and-down. I had definitely done the same to her already, I like blondes, sue me, but it is really, really different when a sexy woman does it to you instead. I know I blushed, and there were a lot of comments and a few titters. Get one thing straight, I am not that good looking. I can get a girlfriend, but not any girl, and I just clam up near the really gorgeous ones. Anyway, Blondie shuffles her sword sash thingy and pistol belt off and drops them on the ground, without looking at them, then undoes the three loops on the front of the jacket. That's how I, and the rest of the crowd, know what colour her undies were. Then she stepped forward and held out her hands, palm upwards. So I put out my hands. Come on, what else was I going to do? Run away? Part of me wishes I had, the rest ..... So she takes hold of my hands, very gently, and steps right up to the barrier (something in my head was willing the barrier to evaporate, but it didn't). She leaned in and put her head next to mine, then she stuck her tongue in my ear. I had heard about that, but never had it done, and it was a hell of a shock. Before I could react however (this is the bit that I didn't tell anyone) she said "Dream of Me". It wasn't the words, although they were definitely prophetic, it was the voice. Deep for a woman, definitely sexy, and something in me recognised it. I hadn't heard it before, you understand, but some ancient bit of me, way down below thinking, reacted like a pet dog being stroked. Probably more like a cat I suppose. It sort of uncoiled and luxuriated in the sound. OK, that sounds really wacko, but that is the nearest description I can give. While my brain was having such fun, she pulled my hands forward, one on her firm, round ass (sorry, must get a grip - oops, a bit Freudian), and the other up on that smooth, very naked back under the coat. She smiled, whispered "If you put out your tongue I will bite it off", grabbed my head with both hands and kissed me. I had never been kissed before. I thought I had, but apparently not, the previous attempts were relegated to sisterly pecks. My lips were overwhelmed, lubricated and then massaged in hot, wet velvet, and they weren't fighting back!

Hang on, needed a cold drink, I try not to think about the kiss too often, though it is in my dreams I think.

I didn't pass out from lack of breath, but it was a close thing when she pulled back, and removed my hands. My hands didn't really want to leave, but hey, I thought, that was definitely a result. Then she said "When the master grants me a servant, I will call, and you will kiss my whip" Right then I think I would have kissed any damn thing she offered, it was only afterwards it seemed a weird thing to say. My inner Tomcat slowly subsided as she stepped back, and slowly (bitch) did up her jacket. Then she very clearly said "Tasty" and licked her lips, one of those licks, slow and wet. Bitch. Again. Another smile, while Mr. Dumb and Stupid stood there, probably with my chin, or maybe my tongue, resting on the barrier. Then she turned, bent over and picked up her weaponry, the metal stuff, not what she was born with. That gave us all a good look at where my hand had been. My other hand had been happy with it's part in the business up to then, but now it was jealous. Then Blondie sashayed off back towards her place, obviously very pleased with herself. I wasn't really paying attention to anything else, although I distinctly heard some woman say "Oh God, I think I just turned Gay", when that bloody whipcrack broke the spell. Blondie froze. Porno Queen was looking sudden death at her, but Blondie was looking at the Master. He was slowly coiling his whip and didn't look enchanted with the whole thing. Well, the sashay disappeared, Blondie scurried over, and went down on one knee, head down and very very subservient. Porn Queen snarled something, and she stiffened a bit, but himself answered in a much calmer tone, and you could see some of the tension ooze out of her. Porn Queen looked away, murder in her eyes, and it crossed my mind that the next security bod to put his hand out was going to lose it. At least. It was peculiar, we could hear what they were saying, and had no idea what it meant, only a guess based on tone and reaction. Like a movie with the sound off and music to set the mood. Anyway, they went back and forth a little, then she perked up, grabbed the hand with the whip and kissed it. I don't know if it was hand or whip, but her words keep coming back hard enough to take a guess. Up she bounced, gave me a dazzling, triumphant smile that nearly stopped my heart, and strode off back to her spot at the back. Then the bitch didn't look at me again. I couldn't take my bloody eyes off her, but she just stood there with a little smile, although her opposite number gave me a look-over and said something. Anyway, that's why I'm not sure exactly what happened next until the whole parade started up again.

It can only have been two or three minutes, but it is the only time they have ever stopped at all. The next time someone tried to slow them down was bloody, it was the parade down the Champs Elysee and French cops have guns. Fat lot of good they did. The newspapers said twenty three police and secret service dead, and a lot very badly cut up, literally. The French were a bit non-committal about any casualties on the other side, but from the results since we can be fairly certain there weren't any. Perhaps the London Premiere was a sort of recce. None of them have ever wandered over to snog a passer-by since either, if they want someone they just take them along. Some people tell me I had a lucky escape. First, a lot of me thinks those that were taken were the lucky ones, and secondly, the rest of me doesn't believe that I have actually escaped. I often feel like one of those hares that were released for the dogs to chase if they couldn't find a wild one. Or a fish put back in one of those ponds so it can be caught again. I am also fairly certain that my inner Tomcat won't let me run if the huntress turns up. He is quiet most of the time, but not in those dreams. Can't remember them, but there is a whip, and Blondie, and I wake up soaked in sweat and wishing I could have stayed asleep. The day after is always hard, I can't concentrate, I want to just pack it all in and go and find her. Every time I think of finding her, I get a real jolt from the subconscious, my deep-down inner whatever. My uncle says its post-hypnotic suggestion, and that if I truly don't want something then no-one can make me do it by hypnosis. Trouble with that is I think I want what's being offered. So I went to a hypnotist, he tried to find something, and he couldn't hypnotise me. He said I wasn't a good subject, and it couldn't be done by a couple of words. So why the dreams? He said it was just a young bloke who had been wound up by a sexy bird, and to get a girlfriend and get over it. I'd love to, but none of the women round here have any effect on me any more.

Anyway, back to the start of it all. The parade got under way, the security guards moved well out of the way and an older bloke did the door opening and ushering in bit. We watched them all disappear through the doors, which was a really nice view, and then the whole lot of us started nattering like washerwomen. Several blokes came over to tell me what a lucky dog I was, ask if I knew her, and did I get a number. Most of them wanted to leave me their number to pass onto her mates, but it was a bit of a shambles as nothing electric was working, and people don't carry pen and paper any more. How many of us actually remember our mobile number, especially if we like to change the phone now and then? Anyway, most of the theories were either a stunt to publicise the film, or someone else bagging a chunk of air time by crashing the party. A Russian billionaire was a popular guess.

A lot of people were just trying to get their phones working, or trying to get to a public phone to call home when they found no-one had a phone to lend them. The crowd was starting to break up a bit, although a lot were staying for the exit show, me among them. Then we heard the sirens, a lot of them and then they went quiet, one after the other. A bit later, a bunch of police, looking a bit baffled, arrived and told us all to stay put. That caused some aggravation, but they said anyone could leave once they had made a statement, so it all quietened down. There was a bit of swearing when a bloke in leathers, yes, very tight ones, appeared out of the back of the rickshaw limo and drove off with it. The back of that thing must have been like the Tardis. From the swearing, it seemed nothing else was working, all the cars and vans had conked out in the adjacent streets. A brain had been applied somewhere, because it was announced that anyone who wanted to go would be able to make calls and get a cab in the next street, and a nice policeman would show them where, presumably after nobbling them for a statement. Turned out you could use a phone a couple of streets over, but not if it had already conked out, and if you brought a good one into the affected area it died. They were fried, chips, batteries, the lot were scrap. There was a huge ruckus about the insurance claims, as some firms claimed an act of God, or an act of war, even though neither were present at the time. Although there is now a growing religious movement claiming they really are Gods. Anyway, in among the profanity from various people, the word started to spread.

Must keep on track, keep drifting off into a sort of daydream. The flickering of the candles and I can feel the moon coming up, and I am sure I can feel her coming. Blondie. She did say "When I call", Did she mean she would come and collect me, or that she would reel me in from wherever? If I was sure where she was, I can't say I wouldn't be headed there. My pride is fighting a losing battle, and if she turns up I doubt I can even put up a struggle. "Kiss my whip" Gods, it eats away in my head, that voice, and every time my id, or whatever, rears up and purrs at the thought. I am not the submissive type, how the hell am I thinking like this? Dream of me? I'm bloody dreaming while I'm still awake!

So I was stood at the barrier, thinking really nice thoughts, when it got chilly, because these two bloody great suits were surrounding me, cutting off the sun. I felt surrounded, anyway, and everyone else backed off. I was very politely invited to join them for a moment, which seemed the smart thing to do, and we went off around the side of the place, and in what must be the stage door. Inside all hell was breaking loose, uniforms and suits with wired ears and big blokes with serious faces all racing around, totally buggered because they were having to actually talk face to face. I was parked in a chair in a small room with a minder, and asked if I would mind waiting a moment. Well yes I would, I really, really wanted to be where Blondie could see me on the way out, and said so. That's when I found out they had all gone. Just stepped out of another door and poof! Waved a bloody wand or cracked a whip or something. Anyway, I sat there and waited, but gradually I started to figure out what all the fuss was. The bloody superstar male lead was missing. Not kidnapped, everyone agreed he went willing, but I doubt his brain was firing on all cylinders. There again, I have a bit of first-hand experience. The Porno Queen had said something to him (Kiss my Whip? Lick my Feet?) and he had followed her like a puppy on a lead. The Master had been masterful with one of the junior starlets, and a policewoman, and they had toddled off as well. It was the policewoman that had everyone's knickers in a twist. A bit of a looker and hard as nails apparently, definitely a rising star and NOT the type to go AWOL. The general opinion about the other two was they would turn up after a dirty weekend somewhere and we would find out what it was all about. I just kept quiet, and hoped they would forget about me. The original object of my desires turned up and any other time I would have tried to at least speak to her, but to be honest she just didn't do it for me any more. Anyway, what a bitch. Complaining that she was lucky not to have been taken, complaining about the lack of security - personally I think she was miffed because Himself took the younger lass and a policewoman instead of her! There was a lot on the news about how her team had bravely defended her but I heard nothing about that at the time, and I was there.

Eventually I was interviewed, it was funny really, the poor bugger was having trouble writing it all down since his tape machine wasn't working. He was using the headed paper from the venue and a cheap biro, and kept stopping and flexing his fingers. Wasn't used to it, well, none of us are. Were. Getting used to it now, electrics aren't really reliable any more, are they? He asked me what I saw, what everyone said, about what everyone else was asked it turned out. Then in came another bod, and the questioning became a lot more precise. They wanted to know what I had done to attract Blondie, although they didn't call her that. I told them I didn't know, because I still don't, maybe it was the drooling. Well not really but I probably looked as if I was about to drool. They had given them all designations, guard four, blonde, was hers, as good as anything I suppose. They wanted me to tell them everything I remembered about her, which made me go a bit hazy for a bit. That girl was intense up close and personal, and details were hard to remember. How would you like to have to describe a barely dressed, very attractive young woman who had thoroughly snogged you to a couple of po-faced suits? 'I wanted to jump her there and then, sod the spectators' isn't what they are after. We worked through what she was wearing, or not wearing, and then they wanted to know what the material was. Soft? Warm? No, that would be her. Flimsy? Definitely. Hell, I'm not Gok Wan, it was clothing, very nice but as a healthy young heterosexual bloke the stuff holding the clothing in shape was my main concern.

What did it feel like, bloody marvellous. Did she appear human? What? Too damn true, and too damn human, the skin was the right temperature I thought, once they asked me, and felt like skin to me. Not that I'm an expert, but I have touched skin before, and how could I tell if it wasn't, my reactions said it was real. What did her breath smell like? Unless there is a bit of a problem with a girl's breath, I can't say I've ever paid attention, and the smell wasn't what I was concentrating on! What did she say? That was easier, although I did find one problem. Every time it came to the 'Dream of Me' bit, my mouth stopped working. I couldn't tell them, and I did try. I could get up to the tongue in ear bit, which got them very excited (strange lives some people lead) but then my mouth skipped a bit. Apparently they had some of the other spectators 'helping' them since a woman kept coming in with bits of paper to compare, but none of them could have heard the dream bit. Or maybe they couldn't talk about it either. Odd that, I can write it down, never thought of that at the time.

Next came a doctor, or someone in a white coat, and she wanted to have a good look at my mouth and ear. Q tips are not as sexy as a hot tongue, as my poor ear could testify by the time she had dug deep enough to get a brain sample. She finally had enough of whatever, and then I went behind a screen for a quick once-over inspection, to see if I had alien bugs or fingerprints on my ass? Nobody wanted to explain and I was a still bit shocky so not quite as bolshy as I might have been another day. My clothes were given a hoovering for moon dust or drugs, and eventually I was allowed to leave with a warning not to talk to anyone else about what happened. Bit bloody stupid that, it was all over the news that night.

Oh gods, the light outside is flickering. It's the only street light that works, maybe it's just finally breaking, after all none of the houses have electric now. Or maybe she is finally coming. I hope nobody manages to contact plod, not after the mess in Brazil. It was a bloody carnival, why did some military genius decide using tanks to try to arrest a few of them was a good idea? When the first armoured car blew up and the rest opened fire they had no idea who they were supposed to be shooting at, everybody was in a costume after all. Hundreds of innocents gunned down, most of the armour melted into scrap, and no sign that they even scratched the real targets. I don't want that around here, half the neighbours are relatives. The Chinese option, I don't think that could happen here, surely not, it's still England. Rumour and some long shots of a mushroom cloud, then a couple of hazy aerial shots of a clean untouched circle in the middle of ruin. The Chinese won't talk, and if they'd got some of them they would be crowing to the world instead of trying to explain where the Olympic stadium had gone.

Anyway, the phones don't work on a good day, probably nobody would get a signal. Unless she is coming, if I stop to think I can feel her, I'm sure I can, bloody sweat breaking out all over and that damn voice. I can remember the smell now all right, but the nearest to a description I can get is that she smelled like a woman. No, it's not a description, it's all my brain can associate with the smell. Better get the rest down, the street light just went, and the radio has gone all static. The papers, when we get them, say that's a sign.

Anyway, I walked away from the premiere, or where it would have been if everything hadn't gone tits-up. There were a lot of people doing the same, and a line of cop cars, pandas and such, across the street. Not to keep us penned in it seemed, it was where they had conked out. Past the line of cars, once a bemused plod had checked my bit of paper to say I had been interviewed, everything was back to normal. My phone still didn't work, or my watch, and later I found that even my credit card was jiggered, but the shops all had lights and electric signs, the traffic lights were going, cars zooming about. Then two steps back and it was all dead. Well, the electrics were, and still are. Tills, computers, security cameras, phone boxes. The government declared it a disaster area, and bought out the businesses and houses except for a few 'back to nature' types who wanted to be free of civilisation. Nobody knew that at the time so I wandered away until I found a cab and went back to my digs. The day is not too clear, not to me or anyone else who was there. Either we were all sprayed with loopy juice or sucked up into spaceships and most of the day erased. Some never recovered, they ended up in homes. I don't remember going to bed, but I remember the dreams. Not the details, just the waking up sweating and trying to stay asleep, that bloody voice, and half-memories of hot, wet, velvet lips.

Shit, it's getting worse, my memory always gets a bit intense if I let it, but this is something more. The shakes are nearly continuous, and my writing is a bit wobbly. At this rate I'll have to stop anyway, but then I might never get it down. If she comes. Or if she calls me. I'm sure she's coming, that rumble of thunder, maybe that's her, they travel like that sometimes, thunder and lightning and pow, there they are. The Others.

That's what they were called by the papers, and TV until it mostly stopped. The internet still works if the computer does. That's where I picked up what had happened to the missing persons, the two lasses and the star? He turned up after a few days, in the middle of Milton Keynes, on a roundabout, in his boxers. Not many of those pictures were taken, but those few, they were all over the internet. His agent claimed he had been to a party and it was a prank, and he disappeared into a 'rest home'. The police issued a statement that he was 'helping with enquiries' about the two women, and then a reporter got to him (of course). Laid there staring into space unless he heard a woman, then he apologised and promised, more or less anything if 'she' would take him back. Questions about the two women made him very quiet, telling the reporter and his assistant to keep quiet, say nothing, they belonged to the Master. That's where we all got the name. The studio claimed he was under medication when he was interviewed but there was never another interview without 'medication'. I reckon he got a full dose of whatever Blondie shoved in my ear, and brain. The last pics were telephotos of him walking along a beach on a lead behind some woman tricked up like the Porno Queen. Can't have been the real thing, the camera and the *cameraman survived. Shit, wonder if that's what Blondie has in mind for me? If she asks in that voice I can't see me saying no, though up until then I really don't fancy it.*

The women turned up later. Well, not exactly, but a fuzzy telephoto picture of the Brazil fiasco showed a woman who a few colleagues identified as the policewoman on a lead. Her police kit was gone, her hair had grown out, but the ones who sold the story were sure it was her. They were a bit startled as well, the blokes reckoned she had been injected with sexy as they hadn't really looked twice before. A month later she was 'guard three, redhead' with a porn version of Zulu dress when 'they' dropped in on a tourist version of the Zulu dances. All blokes flexing muscles and spears, and girls with no bras. The tourists didn't have any snaps of course, and only one of the Zulus got chopped for trying to stop them taking a selected few away with them, so it barely made the papers. It did get on the internet though, I kept running searches as I have a personal interest in how they treat people, and some of the English tourists recognised her.

Blondie has turned up again at least once, and it doesn't help she was the one who kicked off the North Korean thing. She was filling in the Porn Queen position when somebody tried to stop them recruiting from the marchers, and Blondie went crackers with a big curved blade. Ali Baba scimitar thing. Sword against the entire North Korean military and they didn't touch her, she didn't even resort to the lasers or whatever they've used elsewhere. Just the blade, it didn't make me feel any happier to know she's a wild card. Hundreds of damn reporters, they all agreed on the description and a couple had been at the Premiere where, let's face it, she made sure everyone remembered her. After that one, a lot of big parades were cancelled.

The Zulu thing was about what, the fifth or sixth 'visit'? Might have been some that weren't reported. The internet says Machu Pichu, the Aztec city place, can't be reached now. Planes can't get a clear view, and all the trails have been broken, chunks sliced out of them. It could be earthquakes, or just a load of rubbish, the internet is full of stuff like that, type in 'Others' and duck! There are mixed reports about Stonehenge, and that stone age village up in the Scottish Islands. Lights in the pyramids, which are solid rock, shit like that. There is a cult now, they dress up like the Master, or Mistress.

Yeah, there's a Mistress as well, the buggers are spreading. These cultists reckon our ancient Gods have returned, lines of them wait in likely spots, parades and stuff, stripped off and chained by the neck. The only ones to try to talk to the bastards didn't survive though a couple of the slave types were taken, it seems they don't indulge in casual chat. Must be linguists though, since everyone they were seen to speak to understood all right and trotted off without complaint. Russians, Chinese, Zulus, Brazilians, Egyptians, Yanks, didn't make any difference.

Where was I, oh yes, talking. I left London a couple of days later, couldn't sleep or settle, so I came home. Up here in the Pennines we are away from the big cities, crowds and parades and such. I thought I would be safe, but either she has found me or whatever is getting stronger and I'll end up going to find where she is. I know, you see, the direction, if not the distance, it's like an itch, in my head, it eases when I turn to face her. Should have told someone, plod or the army or maybe the vicar, but it's odd, the itch is mine, I don't want to share her, she's mine. Or more likely, I am hers. Oh no, the fridge has gone, gas fridges were supposed to keep working, or maybe it's a crap fridge. No more cold drinks, tonight will be bad. They never told me if those Q tips had anything on them, I've looked in my ear with a mirror and it looks OK. My mouth hasn't developed any problems, unless I think about hot wet velvet and then it gets lonely. Must stop that, I'll lose it. It's harder now, hard to concentrate, don't know if anyone will find this. Fresh candle, sod the expense, that thunder is nearer, and a flicker of lightning over there, and yes, it's the right direction and the itch is growing stronger. I'm not going out to meet her, I've got some pride left! She'll have to come and get me, it's the least I owe myself. Judging by the ones who have been released, it might be the last thing I do by myself. Those who come back are like the film star, broken inside, apologising, asking to be taken back. Sticking them on a lead with a keeper seems to be the only 'treatment' that helps them, according to the internet. Then again, those who don't come back are starting to show up on leads, or sometimes as armed guards, and they seem happy enough so maybe it won't be so bad. They seem relaxed from the reportss so maybe they at least get to sleep properly. Without dreaming.

Just looked out of the window, the lights down in the village are going out, it's a black stain spreading this way. They are here. She is here. I can hear *the voice now, murmuring away behind my ears, inside my head. 'Dream of me, dream of me.' That ancient something from way before cave-men is answering, and all the civilised bits are flaking away, bit by bit, I know who I am if I think and concentrate, and that I must write this, but it's hard now. Ah, the voice, the feel of skin, and hot velvet, wet velvet, my head,*

Sir

The preceding was discovered on a writing table in the front bedroom of number 8. This was the house that witnesses claim was the target of the latest incursion. Further investigations have revealed the occupant was on our 'most wanted' as he is Contact 1, Vector 1, the only living person known to have spoken to, or touched, one of the 'Others' without being taken. The London police lost track as he was no longer at the address given, and it seems he moved here soon after Event 1, to be near his family. The house is now quarantined as recommended, and the whole village is now a dead spot and will need evacuation if alternative accommodation can be found.

Witnesses have described the 'Others' who came here, it seems that the 'Other Contact 1' has come personally to take him. There is no indication whether this was always planned or as a result of some subsequent event. Although the man did not warn his family, and there was no attempt to flee, he may have been expecting something of this nature, given the enclosed papers. There were only five 'Others', a small incursion, and 'Other Contact 1' appeared to be in command. This may indicate promotion to Mistress status as we have seen in other cases. No other villagers were taken, and no contact was made with anyone else. This seems a targeted incursion, for the purpose of collecting one man, a singular occurrence.

Witnesses state that the 'Others' proceeded up the main road on a floater shaped as a Swan, and stopped outside number 8. There was no attempt at communication, but after a few minutes the man appeared at the front door and walked slowly down the path and approached the floater. The Mistress (provisional) descended and he knelt before her, head bowed, in the classic 'enslavement' posture seen elsewhere. She placed a finger under his chin and 'lifted' him to his feet after attaching a chain around his neck. The Mistress (provisional) then ran her hand, or maybe finger, down his chest cutting or breaking the buttons on his shirt, the first time this has been observed. One witness who could see the man's face described it as 'an angel seeing the Lord'. This may be a similar procedure to that observed being carried out by the Master at Event 1, with the 'Barbarian female slave', witnesses should be re-interviewed where possible. Two of the guards from the floater came round and cut away his clothes except for the boots and boxers, again a classic 'enslavement'. We have retrieved the clothes and as usual they have been sliced by an incredibly sharp blade and there is no trace of what did it on the cloth or leather. He then followed her onto the floater, but instead of kneeling at the rear she had him kneel beside her, with her hand on his head. One witness observed that she treated him 'more like a favourite dog than a human'. This is the first time we have seen this change in behaviour, a full debriefing of all witnesses may be advisable to attempt an understanding of the reasons.

The floater then proceeded to the end of the road, through the wall into a field. The wall was cleanly cut and there is no sign of the stones removed. The usual thunder and lightning commenced, and in the black period between two flashes, the whole entourage went - wherever. Standard departure procedure as observed elsewhere although cutting through into the field is unusual. Examination of the remaining stone in a laboratory is being organised once we have transported it by hand beyond the dead zone.

This was almost a standard incursion, but the small divergences may be significant and expand our understanding of the 'Others' and their motives. Given their increased activity, and the deteriorating infrastructure, please expedite the dispatching of relevant experts and sufficient manpower to carry out a major investigation.

THE HEART OF A HUNTER

or The Old Man, The Hunter, and The Hound

The Old Man was almost in a good mood. At last the long hunt was coming to an end. This was one of the last of his breed, old school, tough as leather and cunning as Fox. It was old age, not just the trap that had finally caught him, but the Old Man had stalked this one for too long to care. Another year and old age might do the job, and the Old Man wanted this one himself, a matter of pride.

Up in the high valleys, an early storm had caught the prey with his companion, the deep snow locking them in a narrow, steep valley. They might still have struggled through the drifts, but the cold snap froze the surface of the snow, not enough to support him, but it made movement into brutal work. The Old Man thought his companion might have left, being lighter the snow crust would have held long enough, but they stayed together. It would kill them both.

It surprised the Old Man, that loyalty. Most of the tamed creatures, those that had sold out for food and shelter, were fickle in their loyalty. But not this one. He moved around the bluff, the pine needles rustling as they were coated in hoar frost. Small branches cracked as the deep cold that moved with him froze their sap, and the small creatures huddled deeper into their burrows as the chill swept through. On the edge of the mist, barely visible, drifted the grey hunters. Silent, watchful, easily keeping pace. Above, Raven had picked up something in the wind, hint of a possible meal. Not this time, the Old Man thought, nothing for you or your followers, Raven. One good blast of killing cold and the body would by entombed in ice until spring. Something for the villagers to talk about, something for them to chew over in the long dark nights next winter.

There, propped up under a big old pine, where the trunk cut the wind and the snow curled round the base and formed a hollow. The Old Man noted the freshly cut branch strapped to his leg, and the glint of the long knife held in the mittened hand, down alongside the leg. Fighting for an edge up to the end. It was almost a shame, this Hunt had livened up many a winter. Bending slightly, the Old Man blew gently. A broad band of ice crystals rose from the snow beneath the tongue of icy mist that drifted towards the hunter. "No!" A guttural snarl, heavily accented. The companion was there, blocking the way, ruff up, teeth bared, breathe pluming. The killing frost moved past and away to either side and dissipated in the undergrowth, its path marked by crackles and the scolding of a startled Jay. The Hound turned from black to white in a moment, icicles forming on his jaw line.

The Old Man laughed. "No?" He said, "no one bids me yea or nay! Stand aside, slave, it is your master I have come for. He is mine - Rules of the Hunt". He raised his head and pursed his lips again.

"No!, Mine!" snarled the hound, "You break the Laws of Hunt." He shook, and the rime flew from him in a rainbow glitter as his coat became black again. Except, the Old Man noted, for the muzzle, where time had left a permanent frosting.

"You dare? What would a slave know of the Laws of Hunt, of the Way of fang and claw? You left the Way when you crawled into the huts of men, begging their food, sleeping by fires, protecting lawful prey from your brothers. You have no right to call on the Law. You are no Hunter, you can barely speak the Tongue. Get out of the way or die with him." Then he paused, and curiosity finally broke past his temper "what Law did I break?"

"This cold, after the early snow," the hound spat. "You may not think much of me, but I can smell your Magic, Old Man. This weather stinks of it"

"So what?" the Old Man asked. "This is a Man, they cheat all the time. Huts to hide in, fires to keep out the cold, they kill trees and tear ground to raise food, and pen the beasts to kill without hunting. A little trick or two to even the odds, no big deal. Now stand aside, I will not ask again."

But Hound was not done. He moved back, covering the hunter with his body. "Not this one," He laughed, tongue lolling out over his teeth, "you know this one. He is Hunter. He does not know the Law or speak the Tongue, but he keeps to the old ways. Long have you stalked him, this my sires sire told me, and he told me, and you know him well. He hunts for need and leaves the tithe for the Raven and Fox, and he kills quicker and cleaner than most. Do you see fire or shelter here? He has his hut in the forest, but does not Squirrel need shelter in the dead of winter, does Bear not have a cosy hole to sleep in? No, you have no excuse for cheating, you could not catch him true, and magic in the Hunt is not the Way." Then the Hound paused, and looked hard at Old Man Winter. "Why are you so set on this? Another winter, and neither of us may be here to tramp all over your woods."

Old Man Winter relaxed a little, impressed by the challenge in spite of himself. Too few would stand against him these days and he did enjoy a bit of an argument now and then. "I suppose I did know that", he admitted. "There are few good ones to Hunt now, most stick close by the hearth when I come a' calling. Suppose I was a bit miffed this one might get the away from me in the end. Fair enough, you caught me, I cheated." He chuckled, frost hoaring the bushes, "but it will make no difference now. The grey hunters will do the job anyway now he is down, so it might be kinder to let me finish the job."

"Not so," said the Hound. "I claim this valley, as Pack. By the Law, and by my blood and bone I claim it, and by your Word, Father. Pack does not trespass without need. Pack does not hunt marked territory. All prey in this valley is mine, and by fang and claw I will hold it." He paused. "Father" Then he threw back his head and howled.

The Old Man looked back. The grey hunters had followed him into the mouth of the valley, loping easily over the crust on the snow. Now they paused, and cast about among the trees marking the edge of the cut. They whined, then the Alpha cocked his leg on the two largest trees, but on the downhill side. He looked hard at the Old Man, then threw back his head and answered the Hound, quickly joined by the rest of the pack. "What" asked the Old Man, "are you frightened by a broken old Hound? Pah! Blood runs thinner these days"

Unperturbed, the Alpha looked past him at the Hound. "Hello, slave", he snarled "ready to try a real hunt yet?"

The hound looked back, then ambled over to a bush and lifted his leg. "Why", he replied "do you know where there are any real hunters?"

The Alpha looked at the Old Man. "Blood doesn't look so thin from here," he said. "Why should we kill this bag of bones and gristle, either of them? Neither of them would be worth chewing, and I notice you have not tried to take his long claw. If you want someone to take your cripples, call Jackal. But you might need a lot of them, and you will have to cripple this pair some more before my craven cousins will dare it."

A young male pushed forward. "I am not frightened of Man, or his slave," he growled. "I will finish them, Old Man." He leapt forward, but the Alpha smashed a shoulder into his flank, and was on him, snarling and nipping. The youngster flattened, throat and belly offered. "Sorry," he whimpered, as the Alpha stepped away and allowed him to slink back through the Pack, tail down. The Alpha looked at the Hound. "Youngsters!" he growled.

The Hound chuffed. "Yes," he replied "we still have to tell them, just because the hunted runs doesn't mean its smart to chase, but now and again one has to try."

"Well", the Alpha said, "we are done here then?"

"I think so," the Hound said, "if you have any problems with this" He indicated the valley, "I will come out to the Wild one night when I haven't got more pressing business, and we can sort it out." A ripple of growls through the waiting Pack, silenced by a glare from the Alpha.

A smaller, slimmer wolf pushed forwards, "from what my aunts tell me, you have come out into the Wild on a few nights already, in the past." The bitch glanced at the Old Man, "she didn't mention thin blood."

"Hoo, yes, those were the days, don't get to howl at the moon so often now." The Hound returned his attention to Alpha, "if one valley is too much, might have to do it one more time."

"I think we can spare one valley, but if not, then perhaps, one day." With that the Alpha turned and, as one, the Pack slipped away into the mist.

"By the fires of summer, you are a crafty old Fox," Old Man Winter cried. "Still, even though you call me Father, I didn't expect them to honour a drop of dog piss. Must be more of the old blood left then I thought. You seem to know each other well enough though, is that how you know the Tongue?"

"The Tongue? What makes you think we ever forgot? My blood has never thinned that far! I learned it at my mothers teat, same as Alpha. How can anyone insult an enemy, or a cousin, or warn them away if they don't understand each other? You should pay a little more attention to your own, even if they have taken up other employers. We are not so very different from the grey hunters, in truth, scratch the black a little, and the grey hunter is still under there."

"You are slaves," spat the Old Man, "chained and collared and dragged into exile. You have been beguiled by easy food and soft beds, soft warm beds in front of fires. Your spirit is gone, snuffed out by soft living and slavery, you are no true kin of the grey hunters."

"No kin, hah! Instead of stamping around in a temper, you should sit and listen one calm night, when the moon is full, listen to us calling back and forth. Sometimes," the Hound said, wistfully, "we sing the old songs with them. Tales from before the coming of man. So," the Hound continued, the edge back in his words. "Since we are so craven, perhaps you should put a chain on me and drag me back to the Wild?"

"Ho, you'd like that," chuckled the Old Man." No thanks, I like the number of fingers I have at the moment. All right, so no one dragged you away, and there is still some fire in your blood." He paused, and leant forward, sniffing. "Hah! A lot more fire than there should be, not much more than a couple of generations back. Enough to make you as biddable as your wilder brothers, it seems." He paused, lost in thought. "The Pack, your brothers, were always my best work. The fastest, fiercest hunters, frightened of no creature, untameable." He leapt to his feet in sudden rage. "Then man took them! Tamed them! Softened them! Broke them! Made them nothing!" The trees swayed in the sudden, raging wind, Raven, Jay and Crow fighting for air and balance, the snow swirling and lashing at the Hound.

"Not so!" snarled Hound, teeth bared, "Not so! We were never taken, we were never broken!"

The wind dropped as suddenly as it had arrived, and the snow drifted back down, but Raven and his cronies stayed high, gently circling. With the Old Man in this sort of mood, a bit of manoeuvring room was preferable. The Old Man slumped down again. "It matters not" he grumped, "done is done, the why doesn't matter"

But the Hound would not let it drop this time. "It matters," he argued, "it matters to me, and even more to you. Is this why you hate man, why you prowl around his cabins in the night, hunt his hunters, break his fences, scatter his herds, flatten his crops? You still rage because he took us? But we went willing," said the Hound, quieter now, "we let him place his collar on us in pride, to mark us as his Pack. Look at me, I do not wear a collar unless we visit a town, and then it is as the mark of his Pack, so all will know. Let it go, Old Man. We only joined a different hunting Pack, one not of your making, but deadly none the less. With Man, the Pack has spread farther and wider than you ever dreamed. The golden cats of the plains and the spotted cats of the jungles have learnt of Pack, much as old stripy did in the first days, and their prey is ours. Man is a Hunter too, but he is the favoured child of Summer. She is a softer mistress, and he needs Pack to hunt the cold lands, the deep Wild out to the edges of the world. Many have forgotten the Way, but deep inside Man is still wild although most are not like this one, and they grow soft, as do too many of my kin. But even in his soft, rich lands to the South, the memory still lives in him and before he destroys the last forest, and drives the Wild to the edges of the world, that will stop him. Already a few speak of stopping the destruction, of the need for more Wild, and they are awakening others.

You like to test yourself? Then admit it, do not cloak it in anger, admit that Man and Hound give you a chance to test your edge. The last real test. Do not cheat to catch an old Hunter and his Hound when they were too quick for you in their prime. It is cheapens your skill."

"But who can I test myself against," the Old Man complained, "once you have gone? How can I let the last ones escape?" He glanced at the Hunter, and was startled to see two puzzled eyes peering out at him, wide in alarm. "No chance now, no escape," he muttered softly. "Sorry, Hound, but he has seen me."

"What, that old excuse, 'Man must never see my face'? scoffed the Hound. "They have a thousand legends of the Old Man of the

Woods, although," he cocked his head, "your feet don't look that big to me! He will put it down to pain and cold, or he will talk of it and the children of men will laugh at him. As for what you will tell everyone else," he continued, "well, every Hunter has a tale of the one that got away. Every Hunter but one. Maybe you should have a tale too! Mind, pride does urge me to ask you to make it a good story"

"But the last one," the Old Man groaned.

"Not so," said the Hound. "Son of his son is Hunter too. Not yet in the winter wood, not deep enough into the Wild to catch your eye, but he will come. When he does, don't expect an easy run. Son of my son hunts with him, and I have told him of your sneaky tricks, as my father told me."

The Old Man brightened. "Not the last? His kin and yours?" A small smile broke through. "Sneaky? Me? Those are the skills of the Hunt, puppy." He glanced at the Hunter, and, fickle as ever, made a decision. "You win, he said," I will take a slow stroll home and work on my story. Although," he added, "I may not need it, I don't think he will make it anyway." He tried one last time. "Come with me," he pleaded, "come back to the Wild, leave the soft, warm huts of man and run again with the Pack."

The Hound laid down, by the man. "I think not," he said. "We are not done yet. Once you are gone, I will dig for dry sticks, and rouse him enough to make a fire. Considering what you did here, I think we can cheat a bit as well. There is a hind down the draw, caught by your trap, and with a fire we will eat well and sleep warm. By dawn, fresh and rested and with meat in our bellies we will be strong enough to make it out. If it comes to it, Hunter will make a sled with a few branches and I will drag him out." The Hound huffed in amusement. "Man has a few good tricks. Tell the grey hunters there will be plenty of fresh meat left, although Raven will no doubt get his share first." He frowned at the Hunter's leg. "Let them know we will not be hunting here again for a while, it is open land unless I claim it again" He growled softly. "If we claim it, for this may be his last Hunt, and I will not Hunt without him"

"But I still don't understand." Old Man Winter asked, still truly puzzled, "what does he give you that I cannot? I gave you fine prey, red meat, rich with life, and the jaws to take it, I made your coat thick and strong to stand my cold. I created you, the swiftest and the fiercest of my hunters, and then I gave you the wilderness to the edges of the world to run free, where Man will never take hold. Why did you desert me for Man?"

The Hound growled. "I did not desert anyone, this man is my Pack. Though I still call you Father, I gave my loyalty to another, freely, as my kin before me. In return, he shared his food when times were hard and prey was scarce, and healed me when I sickened. He kept my pups safe from Bear and Jackal, and raised them with his own children, guarded by his kin and mine while we hunted. When I am too old to hunt, there will be a space by the fire, and I will eat soft meat and play with pups and his kin. I will not reach my end under a bush, starved because my teeth are too rotten and my legs too frail to dine at the kill. At the last, although he will grieve, he will give me the mercy stroke, swift and clean, as he did my father before me. That is not a small gift, Old Man. And then this man gave me something you never had, that you will never understand. Something more precious than all the wild places." The Hound looked the Old Man in the eye. "He gave me his heart."

WOLF AND
THE FAST FOOD BUNNY

The hungry young Wolf trotted through the squishy flooded forest, splosh, splosh, splosh. He rather liked the sound, so he tried a little faster, splishsplishsplish, and then slower, splooosh .... splooosh .... splooosh. He was just considering doing small jumps to see what that sounded like when he was interrupted.

"Oy, stop all that noise, how am I supposed to sleep!" On a thick, low branch just above the mud was a short fat creature, sopping wet through, with ears and whiskers plastered flat. The creature had big teeth and a very cross look on it's face, so Wolf was very polite.

"I am very sorry," he started, "but I was hungry, so I need to go hunting, and Owl told me there were bunny rabbits here. He said they were Wolf food." Wolf looked hard at the bedraggled creature. "Are you a bunny rabbit?"

"Eh, what? Me? Oh no!" The creature looked startled now. "Don't you know what a bunny rabbit looks like?"

"Oh, no, I never saw one, but mummy once described them to me." He looked closer. "Are you sure you are not a bunny?"

"Definitely not! I am a, er, squirrel." The creature smiled confidently. "Not Wolf food, we taste terrible."

"Mummy told me about you, although she said squirrels were skinny," he peered at the plump bottom the creature was trying to hide, "and very fast, and had long bushy tails." Wolf tried unsuccessfully to see the creature's tail. "I don't think yours could be very bushy or it would stick out. Even from behind that suspiciously plump bottom."

"Well not all squirrels are the same, I am from abroad, another country, and I am here visiting relatives. Where I come from the trees are very thick and low, so we don't have to be so skinny, er, slim, so we tend to have, um, big bones." The creature scowled. "Anyway,

didn't your mummy tell you it's rude to comment on somebody's bottom."

Wolf wasn't convinced. That bottom didn't look very bony to him, it looked like, his mouth watered, plumptious lunch. Still, better be sure. "Mummy said that Wolves didn't need manners because we have teeth, so it is up to everyone else to be polite to us. So where is this place you came from? I still haven't seen that tail yet either."

Rabbit, yes, it was Rabbit, was getting a bit nervous now. He thought frantically. "I come from the Isle of Man," he announced triumphantly. "Haven't you heard of the Isle of Man, and Manx cats?"

Wolf thought hard, he had heard something, what was it, oh, yes! "That's it, the cats are odd, not right, ooh, what was it, three legs or something?"

"No you dope," Rabbit replied confidently, "the three leggy thingy is their flag, a Manx Cat has no tail, only a little bit of fluff."

"So it does, I knew it was missing something, Mummy said they probably argued with a Wolf at some time. But," Wolf continued, "how do I know you come from there?"

"Easy" Rabbit twirled triumphantly, "see, no tail, I am a Manx R.. um, Squirrel. ask anyone." Anyone seemed to be hiding, there was no sign of life around except for a couple of little birds high up in the tree.

Wolf was perplexed, he had been almost sure this was a bunny rabbit, though how you were supposed to get the covering off he wasn't sure. It looked well fastened on to him. "you still look a lot like a bunny rabbit to me." He muttered, and his tummy muttered with him.

Rabbit sighed. "Right, what do you know about bunny rabbits? Where do they live?"

Wolf peered dubiously around at the puddles and mud. "In holes in the ground," he replied.

"So" Rabbit asked as reasonably as he could, "where is my hole, if I am a bunny?" It was actually under the puddle just over there, full of dirty water, which was why Rabbit was on this low branch. "Where do squirrels live?" he continued.

"Oh, up a tree. A long way up a tree, because they are," Wolf paused, "skinny."

"Light boned, not skinny," Wolf wondered why the creature sounded annoyed now. "Since I am up a tree, not in a hole, what does that make me?"

"A very big-boned, low climbing squirrel?" It made sort of sense to Wolf, but .... "but if that tail was white and those ears were sticky-up you would look a lot like a bunny. I saw a drawing once."

Rabbit was happy, for the first time, that he was very wet and muddy. Still, he just had to ask. "How come you never saw a bunny rabbit?" he asked. "What did your mummy feed you?"

"Oh, stuff out of boxes, in fact I was wondering how to unwrap you if you were a bunny. The boxes were easy, but I can't see your joins."

"Because I am not food," Rabbit tried to sound as confident as possible. He was really interested now. "Food in boxes? Where did she find, er, hunt these boxes, and what were they."

"They were called Fast Food, I think it was a joke because they never ran away, and she said bunnies were a lot faster. You don't look that fast, now I think about it." The creature looked offended at that, Wolf thought. "She hunted round the back of the Super Market, but I never went there, it was too dangerous, she said." He sniffed. "It must have been, a hunter captured her there."

"Are you sure?" Rabbit had visions of a nice warm, dry wolf den for the night instead of wet mud and damp leaves. "how do you know?"

"Oh," Wolf's ears drooped now, "some people arrived at our den with nets and took all my brothers and sisters away, to a Captive Breeding Programme. Magpie said it was Social Services, they do it to human kids all the time. I was in the bushes annoying the Robin when they came, but I heard everything. I'm not going there!"

"Why not?" Rabbit thought it sounded quite appealing. He wondered if they accepted homeless Rabbits.

"My Dad escaped from there, apparently they feed you and it is a 'cushee number', but Dad said a Wolf is born to be free. I wish he was here, but he said he couldn't stay. He wanted to settle down, but apparently he owed it to Genetic Diversity to travel around a lot. Something he learned about in there. He would have caught rabbits and all sorts of good stuff. And taught me how to open them." Wolf looked really downhearted now. "I really am hungry," he complained, and his tummy complained as well.

Rabbit thought hard. Where could he send this stupid young Wolf where he would either find food or get caught. Plish plish plish plish! What was that? A flash of red fur through the grass, it was Fox! "Look, young fellow, I could help you, but I have my own troubles. Wolves don't eat Squirrels, but Foxes do, and because of my big bones I can't climb these thin trees very well. You see, there are no Manx Foxes, so it doesn't matter at home. But now I will have to run away or hide, otherwise I would help you."

"You really would help me, if Fox left you alone?" The young Wolf looked downright cheerful, though Rabbit couldn't see why. Anyway, he had to decide what to do, run or hide, and neither was very appealing. There wasn't much long grass, and Fox would easily catch him trying to run in the mud.

"Of course I would, but sorry, must go now." Running looked best, maybe Fox would slip in the wet.

"No, no, stay there." The Wolf turned to face Fox as Fox came round a tree, "Mum told me how to deal with this. She said Fox would try to steal our dinner."

More or less true, Rabbit thought, if you knew what dinner looked like.

"Grrrrrrrrrrrr!" Fox stopped sharply, and sized up the situation.

"Hello, young Wolf, I see you found dinner. Would you mind sharing, as I haven't had much luck lately. Maybe a leg?"

"Very funny." Wolf wasn't being fooled. "You want to steal my friend and eat him. Well no, go away. Mummy said I was to tell you that Fox is acceptable food for a Wolf, and I am very hungry at the moment." He showed his very white, very sharp teeth. "In fact, come a bit closer." Wolf had suddenly realised that he had found food that he was certain about.

"Hold on a minute", Fox was actually puzzled. Didn't the idiot know what was on the branch? Rabbit stuck up his ears and stuck out his tongue from behind Wolf, and waved at Fox. "I might be food, but I'm food that bites back, and that rabbit behind you is food that can't bite back. That must be better."

"Oh, no, he's not a bunny, although I thought that at first. I know you will still want to eat him, but he promised to find me food." Wolf took a small step forward. "I think he might have just done that." Rabbit was almost falling off the branch, trying not to laugh at the expression on Fox's face.

"You silly young idiot, look at the ears!" Wolf turned but the ears were firmly plastered down again and the big teeth tucked away. Rabbit concentrated on looking innocent. Behind Wolf, fox took two long, slow steps backwards. "He just put them back down," Fox complained, "look at his tail".

"Wrong colour, he explained that," Wolf replied. "It's no good, Mummy told me all about you. She said you will confuse me and try to trick me. There are lots of stories about it apparently, and she told us some." Wolf bared his teeth. "So I refuse to listen to anything you tell me!" He took a step towards Fox. "Now, about this food thing."

Fox whirled and was gone. Rabbit relaxed, although he noticed that the splishing stopped a short way off. So Fox was lurking. Best to keep this Wolf about for a while, and that warm dry den sounded better and better. Wolf took a bound, then stopped, dejected again. "He got away" he complained.

"You have to be a lot quicker, you should have been practising on things your mummy brought back." Like bunnies, Rabbit thought.

"I did, she did, you pull off the cover and get stuck in, and make sure you lick in the corners for the juice" wolf retorted, "if I could find out where Fast Food lives it would be no problem."

Rabbit heard a little splash out in the bushes. Fox. Hmm. "So," he suggested, "if I could find where Fast Food lives, or get some to come over to you, there would be no need to chase bunnies?"

"Too true!" Wolf was happy again, and his tummy gurgled hopefully. "do you know where it lives?"

"Super Market is near the Black Death," Rabbit wasn't happy. "A lot of R.. Er, Squirrels get killed on that, the big long Black Death. Usually at night. I've seen it, if you step on there, a bright light and squash! Something comes down with a roar and flattens you!" He looked wistful, "there's a huge field full of long, luscious grass over there."

Wolf glanced at him. "I thought Squirrels ate nuts."

"Oh, yes." A pause. "On the Isle of Man we eat grass as well, because of the short fat trees. Not so many nuts. Remember, I told you."

"Oh, yes, I remember. But don't worry, Mummy taught us about the Black Death, she called it wait, look and RUN. We all went down there to practice, I can get over there easy." Wolf stuck up his ears and stood proudly. "come on then."

"If you say so." Rabbit wasn't so sure, but it was either a possible way over the Black Death or wait for Fox. "Let's go then."

Splosh Splosh Splosh and Kerploosh Kerploosh Kerploosh, the pair headed off, although Rabbit, and Wolf when he bothered, could also hear splish splish splish behind them. It didn't take long to reach the Black Death, and Wolf walked boldly up to the edge. "Come on, it's safe just here, just stand by the big tree without branches. Nothing will get you." Rabbit scuttled up close behind Wolf. "When I say run, we run fast," Wolf looked dubiously at Rabbit's bottom, "can your er, big bones move fast?"

"Just watch my tail buster" Rabbit snapped, too annoyed to be frightened. "Now concentrate on the job."

"Wait, wait, wait, ... Run!" and Wolf took off. So did Rabbit, he shot out of there like, well like a rabbit. In no time they were in the long grass at the other side.

"Whoo! Oh, yes! Oh, that smarty pants Fox won't try that in a hurry! Look at all this grass! You are a real pal!" Rabbit was rolling around laughing.

"Yes, and I did watch your tail." It went quiet as Wolf continued, "your fluffy white bunny-like tail." He put a foot on Rabbit and a tooth slipped out. "You lied to me, you are a rabbit, a bunny rabbit food-for-Wolves."

"Maybe", Rabbit squealed, "maybe, but I can still find you Fast Food. Remember, I find you Fast Food, you keep Fox away."

Wolf paused. "But I am hungry now." his tummy growled agreement. "There is no Fast Food here, so bunny food will do. Now, where is your opener?"

"No, wait, Fast Food is just over there, enough for ever and ever!" Rabbit wasn't sure how much food a Wolf needed, but it was worth a try.

Wolf relented, after all, we wasn't sure how to open a bunny, but Fast Food, well, he was an expert with that. They crossed the field, Rabbit not even stopping to try the thick lush grass. A long, high wire mesh fence stretched away to each side, and man-buildings were on the other side. Wolf could smell Fast Food now, and he whined a bit. His tummy whined and grumbled a bit as well. He pawed at the mesh, "we have to go round to the man-gate, but that is how they caught mummy", he whined. "But I have to go, I am sooo hungry now." he turned, and jumped to find Rabbit looking at him through the mesh. From the inside! "Wow, how did you do that? Show me, quick!" He jumped up and down, but Rabbit shook his head.

"You are much too big" he explained, and showed Wolf the place where somebody had squiggled under the wire, and left a hollow bit just big enough for a bunny.

"Oh, no!" Poor wolf was ready to cry, he could smell Fast Food, he could almost see and touch it, but he couldn't reach it. "You are going to leave, aren't you?" he muttered. "It was all a trick, so that I wouldn't eat you. You, Rabbit, are as bad as Fox." Wolf began to seriously consider the Captive Breeding Program, after all there would be food.

Rabbit found he actually cared. For some reason, he couldn't just skip away laughing, as he had meant to. "Look, young Wolf, time for a serious talk." Wolf looked at him despondently. "you need food, but it doesn't have to be bunny." Wolf shook his head, his ears drooping. "I need somewhere warm and safe, because the floods have drowned my burrow." Wolf curled a lip, just a bit, remembering Rabbit pointing out he wasn't in a burrow. Now he knew why. "So if you had Fast Food, you could keep me safe from Fox, and nobody gets eaten," Rabbit concluded, and Wolf raised one ear a bit.

"But I can't get the Fast Food," he pointed out.

"No," Rabbit laughed, "but I can." He paused. "And I will in return for you protecting me from Fox while I eat some grass, and letting me sleep in your den."

Wolf had been slowly raising his ears again. "Really?" Then he slumped, "you are just going to fool me again. Mummy was right, she said I wasn't the sharpest young Wolf, just the fluffiest." He sighed and laid down.

"Just you wait, now what does Fast Food look like?"

"It's a box, a small one like those scattered about, the ones that Seagull is pecking in, but they are empty. I need full ones, I can smell them nearer the man-building. The ones with a picture of a cow or a sheep or a piggy on."

Rabbit set off, and found a huge pile of boxes. There were also some carrots and lettuces, not very fresh but it had been a hard day, and the floods had made finding roots very difficult. He had a quick snack and looked round. Sure enough, some of the boxes had pictures of animals on and smelled like dead things. "Yeuk," he thought, "still, better a dead box thing than a dead Rabbit." He picked up one that wasn't leaking, and dragged it towards the fence, but it wouldn't go through the hole. He tried but it stuck, though Wolf soon fixed that.

Gronch! His teeth bit into the end of the box and he heaved. Most of the box and contents went through the hole, and Rabbit shoved the rest through, careful not to get his foot near those big jaws.

"MMffff, slurp, munch, Mmmm, more please" Wolf growled through the mouthfuls of drippy red stuff. Rabbit gulped, he had forgotten just what a Wolf could do while wandering around with this one. He bounced off quickly, and brought several more back, snacking on some of the best veggies in between trips. This was a fantastic place! There was only one frightening moment, when a Man came round the corner. Rabbit sat very still and watched, ready to run, but the Man just showed his teeth and went inside.

"Hey, Charlie," the man called, "I swear I just saw a rabbit with a box of burgers!"

"Yeah, sure" Charlie laughed, "better watch out for vampire wererabbits on the night shift. At least that Wolf has gone now though." They both laughed.

Eventually Wolf rolled over, his tummy a tight round bump. He burped, and his tummy rumbled, but it was a happy rumble now. He dozed for a bit, and Rabbit topped up his own tummy on lush grass, keeping close to his protector. Some of the resident bunnies had hopped over to chase him off, but the sight of Wolf kept them well away. Bonus! When Wolf woke up, they went back across the Black Death, "wait, wait, wait, ready, ...RUN!" Then they went back through the flooded forest, Splosh Splosh Kerploosh Kerploosh Splosh Kerploosh. Eventually they went up the rocky hill, and there, tucked away behind a boulder, was a snug, warm, dry den, where they curled up, exhausted, and slept.

So if you are driving along the Black Death, and see a Wolf and a Rabbit dash across, look closely. Maybe, just maybe, the Wolf is chasing the Rabbit, but maybe he is just making sure his friend crosses safely. If you see a despondent Fox sat watching them, this is almost certainly our two friends. If you see a Wolf and a Rabbit with bulging tummies crossing the Black Death together, you will know for sure. Don't tell anyone though, or the Captive Breeding Program will be over there looking for the elusive young Wolf, and then the Fox will have his Rabbit dinner!

ABOUT THE AUTHOR

This collection of poems contains some very personal verses and some which may have a broader appeal. The poems vary from four lines to over four pages, the content veers from love poems through dragons and dancing kangaroos to some that are a little more serious and a few weepies.

Having written poetry all his life on scrap paper and cigarette packets, which were quickly lost, about five years ago John's hands finally insisted that a computer was better for his finger joints. The computer didn't lose the poems so a collection grew, and after some encouragement from his brother and the Ark Animal Rescue, he sent a few off to a competition run by United Press. Some were published and now over a score are in print, hidden within many different poetry books, while the collection on his laptop now holds well over two hundred.

John's daughter Joy thought it would be a good idea if his poetry was printed up for John's grandchildren to read in the future, and this is the second instalment. Time will tell whether Jonty and Daisy read them. The first offering was published as Pawprints on My heart in 2013, mainly about cats and dogs.

John now lives in the North Lincolnshire countryside with Scooby the rescue Staffy X. Huxley Pigge, Maybelline, Florence, Misty and Bobby B. (the furry republic) lead them both a dog's life and 'help' John when his typing is interfering with food or cuddles. If his fingers and eyes hold out there will no doubt be another selection in a few years time, inspired by their antics, those of their furry friends or life in general. Before then he may find the courage to publish a collection of his short stories or one of the fictional novels he has written.